SUPER

a selection

16th Century to the 20th Century

Other books edited by Michael Hayes

THE SUPERNATURAL SHORT STORIES OF
ROBERT LOUIS STEVENSON

THE SUPERNATURAL SHORT STORIES OF
SIR WALTER SCOTT

THE SUPERNATURAL SHORT STORIES OF
CHARLES DICKENS

THE FANTASTIC TALES OF FITZ-JAMES O'BRIEN

SUPERNATURAL POETRY

a selection
16th Century to the 20th Century

Selected and edited with an introduction by

Michael Hayes

JOHN CALDER
LONDON

First published in Great Britain 1978 by
John Calder (Publishers) Ltd.,
18 Brewer Street, London W1R 4AS

ISBN 0 7145 3677 6 Cased

Typeset in 9 point Theme by Specialised Offset Services Ltd., Liverpool. Printed by M & A Thomson Litho Ltd., East Kilbride, Scotland. Bound by Hunter & Foulis Ltd., Edinburgh.

ACKNOWLEDGMENTS

For permission to reproduce copyright poems I am indebted to the following: The Literary Trustees of Walter de la Mare, and The Society of Authors as their representative for 'The Listeners' from The Complete Poems of Walter de la Mare; The National Trust and the Macmillan Co. of London and Basingstoke for 'The Sack of the Gods' from The Naulahka, 1892, by Rudyard Kipling; M.B. Yeats, Miss Anne Yeats, and the Macmillan Co. of London and Basingstoke, for 'The Stolen Child' from The Collected Poems of W.B. Yeats. I must also record my grateful thanks for all the assistance and courtesy extended to me by the staffs of The British Library, London WC1., The Central Library, Kensington, London W.8., The County Library, Exeter, Devon, and The National Library of Ireland, Dublin.

To my wife
Arlette
Like always – with love

CONTENTS

INTRODUCTION

The poet's eye, in a fine frenzy rolling,
Doth glance from heaven to earth, from earth to heaven,
And, as imagination bodies forth
The forms of things unknown, the poet's pen
Turns them to shapes, and gives to airy nothing
A local habitation and a name.

William Shakespeare
A Midsummer Night's Dream

It is obvious that you need not believe in Ghoulies and Ghosties and Long-legged Beasties and Things that go Bump in the Night in order to enjoy supernatural poetry. In fact, such an attitude of mind will put you in the select company of most – if not all – of the poets presented in this collection. They may not have lent credence to the weird and unearthly, but found dramatic, poetic material in it, and fashioned it to their own artistic purpose.

During the latter half of the 17th century, the cold reasoning and rational thinking of Thomas Hobbes – re-asserted by John Locke and others – came as a salutary reaction against the superstitious excesses of the Past, but had the unhappy effect of virtually eliminating the marvellous from all poetic composition. Close on a century later, Richard Hurd, surveying the damage in his *Letters on Chivalry and Romance*, 1762, lamented the loss of a 'world of fine fabling.' Later still, Leigh Hunt rightly accused Hobbes of a 'wonderful dimness of discernment in poetic matters.' Nevertheless, the supernatural in poetry gradually reappeared and survived. The poets simply side-stepped the 'mere reasoners' – as Shelly scornfully referred to them – and let their imaginative powers create fresh spells. They gave us back the stuff dreams and nightmares are made of in that vast *terra incognita* of our own minds.

Despite the fact that reason and enlightenment tend to dismiss occult phenomena as mere fantasy, the mind of man is curiously inclined and has always been receptive to things supernatural – a perennial fascination for ghosts and monstrous beings, superstitions, witches, spells and incantations, and weird happenings in strange, eerie places, fulfilling a mysterious craving which is present in us all. Oliver Goldsmith, writing *On Deceit and Falsehood* in The Bee, 1759, aptly qualifies this: 'We have a *wondering quality* within us, which finds huge gratification when we see strange feats done, and cannot see the doer or the cause. Such actions are sure to be attributed to some witch or demon ... It is, therefore, one of the most unthankful offices in the world, to go about to expose the mistaken notion of witchcraft and spirits; it is robbing mankind of a *valuable imagination*, and of the *privilege of being deceived*.' (Italics mine.) In today's 'enlightened' world, plagued with insecurity and wearisome complexities, senseless wars and mindless violence, it is interesting to note that, while the latest deep-space probe, having become a reality, will cause but a passing stir, millions of people seek to gratify their 'wondering quality' by way of supernatural horror films in the cinema and on television, bestselling novels dealing with satanic possession, vampirism, telekinesis, and countless anthologies of tales of the occult and the macabre. Supernatural prose, it seems, was never more in demand. Yet, poetry, one of our oldest and most enduring pleasures, can tell a story just as well, though differently, with a unique intensity lacking in prose.

The Unknown, mirrored in poetry, has many faces, each poet reflecting his own strange vision of events beyond his common experience.

Shakespeare, who lived in an age of widespread belief in witchcraft and the inexplicable, was perfectly at ease writing about witches and ghosts, and the pure enchantment of fairyland in *A Midsummer Night's Dream*:

You spotted snakes with double tongue,
Thorny hedgehogs, be not seen:
Newts and blindworms, do no wrong,
Come not near our Fairy Queen.

Aside from a youthful attempt at macabre poetry in *Fair Elenor*, there emerged from William Blake's teeming imagination a supernaturalism of a far higher order, of terrifying cosmic proportions, which he introduced into his symbolic works:

Lo, a Shadow of Horror is risen
In eternity! unknown, unprolific,
Self-closed, all-repelling. What Demon

Hath formed this abominable Void,
This soul-shuddering vacuum?

In the realm of supernatural poetry the magnificence of Samuel Taylor Coleridge is forever sealed in one complete poem, *The Rime of the Ancient Mariner* with its horror-infested seas; and two fragments – the vampire-haunted *Christabel*, and the mystical *Kubla Khan*. It is inconceivable to imagine these ever being surpassed:

Beneath the lamp the lady bowed,
And slowly rolled her eyes around;
Then drawing in her breath aloud,
Like one that shuddered, she unbound
The cincture from beneath her breast:
Her silken robe, and inner vest,
Dropt to her feet, and full in view,
Behold! her bosom and half her side –
A sight to dream of, not to tell!
O shield her! shield sweet Christabel!

A great deal of supernatural horror poetry was written by second-rate poets during the time-span of this collection. They employed the grisliest ingredients – hideous beings, shrieking fiends, maggot-infested skulls, open graves giving up the mouldy dead – gruesomeness personified. On reading it now, it tends within moments to numb the reason without stimulating the imagination. Thankfully it has faded from sight. Matthew Gregory Lewis will always be remembered for his classic Gothic novel, *The Monk*, which contains the ballad of *Alonzo the Brave and Fair Imogene*. I have included it here as, perhaps, the best example of this type of *verse macabre*:

His vizor was closed, and gigantic his height,
  His armour was sable to view;
All pleasure and laughter were hushed at his sight;
The dogs, as they eyed him, drew back in affright,
  The light in the chamber burnt blue.

Dante Gabriel Rossetti belonged to the world of romance, and his love of the marvellous imbued his poetry. His fascination for all things mysterious and supernatural pervades his chilling litany of relentless evil, *Sister Helen*:

'Ah! what white thing at the door has cross'd,
Sister Helen?
Ah! what is this that sighs in the frost?'
'A soul that's lost as mine is lost,
Little Brother!'
(O Mother, Mary Mother,
Lost, lost, all lost, between Hell and Heaven!)

The singular purpose of the supernatural in literature is to instil a feeling of unnamed dread, or immediate fear, or a sense of awe – certainly not pity. Yet, William Sharp drew unutterable sadness and wonderment from the phantasmal revelry of the spirits of the youths and maidens who died before fulfilling their earthly desires – *The Willis Dancers*:

Swift, swifter, grows the mystic dance
More wild, more wild, each fierce embrace:
The woe of death's inheritance
Gleams ghastly on each wildered face.

These are but a few examples which demonstrate the extent and diversity of the poetic imagination at work in some of the greatest poets, as well as the almost forgotten. Through individual styles, techniques and inventions, they have invested their unusual material with a haunting beauty which has enriched our literature of the supernatural. And it is here, I feel compelled to add: Rest easy, Bishop Hurd, we never did lose that 'world of fine fabling.'

Poetry anthologies are legion and cover a wide variety of subjects – love, nature, childhood, humour, romantic verse, mystical verse, and so on. But supernatural poetry has remained, appropriately, in the shadows. The prime reason which prompted me to put this collection together was obvious and simple – it had never been done before. It is in no sense an academic work and its main purpose is to entertain and give pleasure. It is not aimed at literary scholars, but at all those people who only remember poetry through the tedium of insensitive schooldays, and were glad to finish with it forever.

The selection is a personal one and – with extent in mind – the omission of anonymous ballads and translations deliberate. On the other hand, taking the supernatural in its widest meaning, I have included a few examples of allegory and fairy poetry. The chronological order is a natural one, and best shows mankind's enduring fascination for the supernatural through five centuries.

Seventy years ago, Andrew Lang wrote: 'Why, as science becomes more cock-sure, have men and women become more and more fond of old follies, and more pleased with the stirring of ancient dread within their veins? As the visible world is measured, mapped, tested, weighed, we seem to hope more and more that a world of invisible romance may not be far from us, or, at least, we care more and more to follow fancy into these airy regions.' His words are still valid today.

Heeding that memorable prompt of Samuel Taylor Coleridge where he requests you to wilfully suspend your disbelief for the moment, it is time to indulge your 'privilege of being deceived' and disinherit reality with its deadening daily routine. Loosen your grip on the here-and-now and cross over effortlessly into the alluring, shadowy world of the Beyond – sometimes enchanting, sometimes frightening – where awaits

A wild weird clime that lieth, sublime,
Out of Space – out of Time.

Michael Hayes

EDMUND SPENSER
born 1552? : died 16 January 1599

Night and the Witch Duessa

Then to her iron waggon she betakes,
And with her bears the foul well-favour'd witch:
Through mirksome air her ready way she makes.
Her twofold team (of which two black as pitch,
And two were brown, yet each to each unlich)
Did softly swim away, nor ever stamp
Unless she chanc'd their stubborn mouths to twitch;
Then, foaming tar, their bridles they would champ,
And trampling the fine element would fiercely ramp.

So well they sped, that they be come at length
Unto the place whereas the Paynim lay,
Devoid of outward sense and native strength,
Cover'd with charmed cloud from view of day
And sight of men, since his late luckless fray.
His cruel wounds, with cruddy blood congeal'd,
They binden up so wisely as they may,
And handle softly, till they can be heal'd:
So lay him in her chariot, close in night conceal'd.

And, all the while she stood upon the ground,
The wakeful dogs did never cease to bay;
As giving warning of th' unwonted sound
With which her iron wheels did them affray,
And her dark grisly look them much dismay.
The messenger of death, the ghastly owl,
With dreary shrieks did also her bewray;
And hungry wolves continually did howl
At her abhorred face, so filthy and so foul.

Then turning back in silence soft they stole,
And brought the heavy corse with easy pace
To yawning gulf of deep Avernus' hole.

By that same hole, an entrance, dark and base,
With smoke and sulphur hiding all the place,
Descends to hell: there creature never pass'd
That back returned without heavenly grace;
But dreadful Furies which their chains have brast,
And damned sprites sent forth to make ill men aghast.

By that same way the direful dames do drive
Their mournful chariot fill'd with rusty blood,
And down to Pluto's house are come belive;
Which passing through, on every side them stood
The trembling ghosts with sad amazed mood,
Chatt'ring their iron teeth, and staring wide
With stony eyes; and all the hellish brood
Of fiends infernal flock'd on ev'ry side,
To gaze on earthly wight that with the Night durst ride.

from *The Faerie Queen, Book 1, Canto 5*

MICHAEL DRAYTON
born 1563: died 23 December 1631

Knight in Armour

And quickly arms him for the field,
A little cockle-shell his shield,
Which he could very bravely wield,
   Yet could it not be pierced.
His spear a bent both stiff and strong,
And well-near of two inches long;
The pile was of a horse-fly's tongue,
   Whose sharpness naught reversed.

And puts him on a coat of mail,
Which was of a fish's scale,

That when his foe should him assail,
  No point should be prevailing.
His rapier was a hornet's sting,
It was a very dangerous thing:
For if it chanced to hurt the King,
  It would be long in healing.

His helmet was a beetle's head,
Most horrible and full of dread,
That able was to strike one dead,
  Yet did it well become him:
And for a plume, a horse's hair,
Which being tossed with the air,
Had force to strike his foe with fear,
  And turn his weapon from him.

Himself he on an earwig set,
Yet scarce he on his back could get,
So oft and high he did corvet,
  Ere he himself could settle:
He made his turn, and stop, and bound,
To gallop, and to trot the round,
He scarce could stand on any ground,
  He was so full of mettle.

from *Nymphidia*

WILLIAM SHAKESPEARE
baptized 26 April 1564 : died 23 April 1616

Fairy Song

TITANIA
Come, now a roundel and a fairy song;
Then, for the third part of a minute, hence;
Some to kill cankers in the musk-rose buds;

Some war with rere-mice for their leathern wings,
To make my small elves coats; and some keep back
The clamorous owl, that nightly hoots and wonders
At our quaint spirits. Sing me now asleep;
Then to your offices, and let me rest.

FAIRIES SING
You spotted snakes with double tongue,
Thorny hedgehogs, be not seen;
Newts and blindworms, do no wrong,
Come not near our Fairy Queen.
Philomel, with melody
Sing in our sweet lullaby;
Lulla, lulla, lullaby, lulla, lulla, lullaby!
Never harm,
Nor spell, nor charm,
Come our lovely lady nigh;
So, good night, with lullaby.

FIRST FAIRY
Weaving spiders, come not here;
Hence, you long-legged spinners, hence!
Beetles black, approach not near;
Worm nor snail, do no offence.
Philomel, with melody
Sing in our sweet lullaby;
Lulla, lulla, lullaby, lulla, lulla, lullaby!
Never harm,
Nor spell, nor charm,
Come our lovely lady nigh;
So, good night, with lullaby.

SECOND FAIRY
Hence, away! now all is well:
One aloof stand sentinel.

from *A Midsummer Night's Dream Act 2, Scene 2*

BEN JONSON
born 11 June 1572 : died 6 August 1637

The Witches' Song

HAG
Sisters, stay, we want our Dame;
Call upon her by her name,
And the charm we use to say,
That she quickly anoint, and come away.

Charm 1
Dame, Dame, the watch is set:
Quickly come, we all are met.
From the lakes, and from the fens,
From the rocks, and from the dens,
From the woods, and from the caves,
From the churchyards, from the graves,
From the dungeon, from the tree
That they die on, here are we.

Charm 2
The weather is fair, the wind is good,
Up Dame, o' your horse of wood:
Or else, tuck up your gray frock,
And saddle your goat, or your green cock,
And make his bridle a bottom of thrid,
To roll up how many miles you have rid.
Quickly come away
For we, all, stay.

Charm 3
The owl is abroad, the bat, and the toad,
  And so is the cat-a-mountain,
The ant, and the mole sit both in a hole,
  And frog peeps out o' the fountain;
The dogs, they do bay, and the timbrels play,
  The spindle is now a-turning;

The moon it is red, and the stars are fled,
  But all the sky is a-burning:
The ditch is made, and our nails the spade,
With pictures full, of wax, and of wool;
Their livers I stick with needles quick;
There lacks but the blood, to make up the flood.
    Quickly Dame, then, bring your part in,
    Spur, spur, upon little Martin,
    Merrily, merrily, make him sail,
    A worm in his mouth, and a thorn in his tail,
    Fire above, and fire below,
    With a whip i' your hand, to make him go.
      O, now she's come!
      Let all be dumb ...

DAME
Then fall to.
But first relate me, what you have sought,
Where you have been, and what you have brought.

FIRST HAG
I have been, all day, looking after
A raven, feeding upon a quarter;
And, soon, as she turn'd her beak to the south,
I snatch'd this morsel out of her mouth.

SECOND HAG
I have been gathering wolves hairs,
The mad dogs foam, and the adders ears;
The spurging of a dead man's eyes,
And all since the evening star did rise.

THIRD HAG
I, last night, lay all alone
O' the ground, to hear the mandrake groan;
And pluckt him up, though he grew full low;
And, as I had done, the cock did crow.

FOURTH HAG
And I ha' been choosing out this skull,

From charnel houses, that were full;
From private grots, and public pits,
And frighted a sexton out of his wits.

FIFTH HAG
Under a cradle I did creep,
By day; and, when the child was asleep,
At night, I suck'd the breath; and rose,
And pluck'd the nodding nurse by the nose.

SIXTH HAG
I had a dagger: what did I with that?
Kill'd an infant, to have his fat.
A piper it got, at a church-ale,
I bade him, again blow wind i' the tail.

SEVENTH HAG
A murderer, yonder, was hung in chains,
The sun and the wind had shrunk his veins;
I bit off a sinew, I clipp'd his hair,
I brought off his rags, that danc'd i' the air.

EIGHTH HAG
The screech-owl's eggs, and the feathers black,
The blood of the frog, and the bone in his back,
I have been getting; and made of his skin
A purset, to keep Sir Cranion in.

NINTH HAG
And I ha' been plucking (plants among)
Hemlock, henbane, adders-tongue,
Night-shade, moon-wort, libbards-bane;
And twice, by the dogs, was like to be tane.

TENTH HAG
I, from the jaws of a gardiner's bitch,
Did snatch these bones, and then leap'd the ditch;
Yet went I back to the house again,
Kill'd the black cat, and here's the brain.

ELEVENTH HAG
I went to the toad, breeds under the wall,
I charm'd him out, and he came at my call;
I scratch'd out the eyes of the owl before,
I tore the bat's wing; what would you have more?

DAME
Yes, I have brought, to help our vows,
Horned poppy, cypress boughs,
The fig-tree wild, that grows in tombs,
And juice, that from the larch-tree comes,
The basilisk's blood, and the viper's skin:
And, now, our orgies let's begin ...

DAME
Come, let a murmuring charm resound,
The whilst we bury all, i' the ground.
But first, see every foot be bare;
And every knee.

HAG
Yes, Dame, they are.

Charm 4

Deep, O deep, we lay thee to sleep;
We leave thee drink by, if thou chance to be dry;
Both milk, and blood, the dew, and the flood.
We breathe in thy bed, at the foot, and the head;
We cover thee warm, that thou take no harm:
And when thou dost wake,
  Dame earth shall quake,
  And the houses shake,
  And her belly shall ake,
  As her back were brake,
  Such a birth to make,
  As is the blue drake:
  Whose form thou shall take.

DAME
Never a star yet shot!
Where be the ashes?

HAG
Here i' the pot.

DAME
Cast them up; and the flint stone
Over the left shoulder bone:
Into the west.

HAG
It will be best.

Charm 5

The sticks are a-cross, there can be no loss,
The sage is rotten, the sulphur is gotten
Up to the sky, that was i' the ground.
Follow it then, with our rattles, round;
Under the bramble, over the brier,
A little more heat will set it on fire:
Put it in mind, to do it kind,
Flow water, and blow wind.
Rouncy is over, robble is under,
A flash of light, and a clap of thunder,
A storm of rain, another of hail.
We all must home, i' the egg-shell sail;
The mast is made of a great pin,
The tackle of cobweb, the sail as thin,
And if we go through and not fall in ...

Charm 6

Bark dogs, wolves howl,
Seas roar, woods roll,
Clouds crack, all be black,
But the light our charms do make ...

Charm 7

Black go in, and blacker come out;
At thy going down, we give thee a shout.
Hoo!
At they rising again, thou shalt have two,
And if thou dost what, we would have thee do,
Thou shalt have three, thou shalt have four,
Thou shalt have ten, thou shalt have a score.
Hoo! Har! Har! Hoo!

Charm 8

A cloud of pitch, a spur, and a switch,
To haste him away, and a whirlwind play,
Before, and after, which thunder for laughter,
And storms for joy, of the roaring boy;
His head of a drake, his tail of a snake.

Charm 9

About, about, and about,
Till the mist arise, and the lights fly out,
The images neither be seen, nor felt;
Sprinkle your liquors upon the ground,
And into the air; around, around.
  Around, around,
  Around, around,
  Till a musique sound,
  And the pace be found,
  To which we may dance,
  And our charms advance.

from *The Masque of Queens*

ROBERT HERRICK
baptized 24 August 1591 : buried 15 October 1674

The Hag

The Hag is astride,
This night for to ride;
The Devil and she together:
Through thick, and through thin,
Now out, and then in,
Though ne'r so foul be the weather.

A thorn or a burr
She takes for a spur:
With a lash of a bramble she rides now,
Through brakes and through briars,
O'er ditches, and mires,
She follows the Spirit that guides now.

No beast, for his food,
Dares now range the wood;
But hush't in his lair he lies lurking:
While mischiefs, by these,
On land and on seas,
At noon of night are a-working.

The storm will arise,
And trouble the skies;
This night, and more for the wonder,
The ghost from the tomb
Affrighted shall come,
Called out by the clap of the thunder.

JOHN MILTON
born 9 December 1608 : died 8 November 1674

Satan Arises

Thus Satan, talking to his nearest mate,
With head up-lift above the wave, and eyes
That sparkling blazed; his other parts besides
Prone on the flood, extended long and large,
Lay floating many a rood; in bulk as huge
As whom the fables name of monstrous size,
Titanian, or Earth-born, that warred on Jove
Briareos or Typhon, whom the den
By ancient Tarsus held; or that sea-beast
Leviathan, which God of all his works
Created hugest that swim the ocean stream:
Him, haply, slumbering on the Norway foam,
The pilot of some small night-foundered skiff
Deeming some island, oft, as seamen tell,
With fixed anchor in his scaly rind
Moors by his side under the lee, while night
Invests the sea, and wished morn delays:
So stretched out huge in length the arch-fiend lay
Chained on the burning lake: nor ever thence
Had risen, or heaved his head; but that the will
And high permission of all-ruling Heaven
Left him at large to his own dark designs;
That with reiterated crimes he might
Heap on himself damnation, while he sought
Evil to others; and, enraged, might see
How all his malice served but to bring forth
Infinite goodness, grace, and mercy, shown
On man by him seduced; but on himself
Treble confusion, wrath, and vengeance poured.
Forthwith upright he rears from off the pool
His mighty stature; on each hand the flames,
Driven backward, slope their pointing spires, and, rolled
In billows, leave in the midst a horrid vale.

Then with expanded wings he steers his flight
Aloft, incumbent on the dusky air,
That felt unusual weight; till on dry land
He lights, if it were land that ever burned
With solid, as the lake with liquid fire;
And such appeared in hue, as when the force
Of subterranean wind transports a hill
Torn from Pelorus, or the shattered side
Of thundering Aetna, whose combustible
And fuel'd entrails thence conceiving fire,
Sublimed with mineral fury, aid the winds,
And leave a singed bottom all involved
With stench and smoke: such resting found the sole
Of unblest feet. Him followed his next mate:
Both glorying to have 'scaped the Stygian flood
As gods, and by their own recovered strength,
Not by the sufferance of supernal power.

from *Paradise lost: Book 1*

The Guardians of the Gates of Hell

Through many a dark and dreary vale
They passed, and many a region dolorous,
O'er many a frozen, many a fiery Alp,
Rocks, caves, lakes, fens, bogs, dens, and shades of death
A universe of death; which God by curse
Created evil, for evil only good;
Where all life dies, death lives, and nature breeds,
Perverse, all monstrous, all prodigious things,
Abominable, inutterable, and worse
Than fables yet have feigned, or fear conceived,
Gorgons, and hydras, and chimeras dire.
Meanwhile, the adversary of God and man,
Satan, with thoughts inflamed of highest design,
Puts on swift wings, and towards the gates of hell
Explores his solitary flight: sometimes
He scours the right hand coast, sometimes the left;

Now shaves with level wing the deep, then soars
Up to the fiery concave towering high.
As when far off at sea a fleet descried
Hangs in the clouds, by equinoctial winds
Close sailing from Bengala, or the isles
Of Ternate and Tidore, whence merchants bring
Their spicy drugs: they on the trading flood,
Through the wide Ethiopian to the Cape,
Ply stemming nightly toward the pole: so seemed
Far off the flying fiend. At last appear
Hell-bounds, high reaching to the horrid roof,
And thrice threefold the gates: three folds were brass,
Three iron, three of adamantine rock
Impenetrable, impaled with circling fire,
Yet unconsumed. Before the gates there sat
On either side a formidable shape;
The one seemed woman to the waist, and fair;
But ended foul in many a scaly fold
Voluminous and vast – a serpent armed
With mortal sting: about her middle round
A cry of hell-hounds never-ceasing barked
With wide Cerberean mouths full loud, and rung
A hideous peal; yet, when they list, would creep,
If aught disturbed their noise, into her womb,
And kennel there; yet there still barked and howled,
Within unseen. Far less abhorred than these
Vexed Scylla, bathing in the sea that parts
Calabria from the hoarse Trinacrian shore:
Nor uglier follow the night-hag, when, called
In secret, riding through the air she comes,
Lured with the smell of infant blood, to dance
With Lapland witches, while the labouring moon
Eclipses at their charms. The other shape,
If shape it might be called that shape had none
Distinguishable in member, joint, or limb;
Or substance might be called that shadow seemed,
For each seemed either: black it stood as night,
Fierce as ten Furies, terrible as hell,
And shook a dreadful dart; what seemed his head,
The likeness of a kingly crown had on.

Satan was now at hand, and from his seat
The monster moving onward came as fast
With horrid strides; hell trembled as he strode.

from *Paradise Lost: Book 2*

WILLIAM BLAKE
born 28 November 1757 : died 12 August 1827

Lo, a Shadow of Horror is Risen

1
Lo, a Shadow of Horror is risen
In Eternity! unknown, unprolific,
Self-closed, all-repelling. What Demon
Hath formed this abominable Void,
This soul-shuddering Vacuum? Some said
It is Urizen. But unknown, abstracted,
Brooding, secret, the dark Power hid.

2
Times on times he divided, and measured
Space by space in his ninefold darkness,
Unseen, unknown; changes appeared
Like desolate mountains, rifted furious
By the black winds of perturbation.

3
For he stove in battles dire,
In unseen conflictions with Shapes,
Bred from his forsaken wilderness,
Of beast, bird, fish, serpent, and element,
Cumbustion, blast, vapour, and cloud.

4
Dark, revolving in silent activity,
Unseen in tormenting passions,
An Activity unknown and horrible,
A self-contemplating Shadow,
In enormous labours occupied.

5
But Eternals beheld his vast forests;
Ages on ages he lay, closed, unknown,
Brooding, shut in the deep; all avoid
The petrific, abominable Chaos.

6
His cold horrors, silent, dark Urizen
Prepared; his ten thousands of thunders,
Ranged in gloomed array, stretch out across
The dread world; and the rolling of wheels,
As of swelling seas, sound in his clouds,
In his hills of stored snows, in his mountains
Of hail and ice; voices of terror
Are heard, like thunders of autumn,
When the cloud blazes over the harvests.

from *The Book of Urizen: Ch 1*

The Vast World of Urizen Appears

1
They saw his pale visage
Emerge from the darkness, his hand
On the rock of Eternity unclasping
The Book of brass. Rage seized the strong –

2
Rage, fury, intense indignation,
In cataracts of fire, blood, and gall,
In whirlwinds of sulphurous smoke,

And enormous forms of energy,
In living creations appeared,
In the flames of eternal fury.

3
Sundering, darkening, thundering,
Rent away with a terrible crash,
Eternity rolled wide apart,
Wide asunder rolling;
Mountainous, all around
Departing, departing, departing,
Leaving ruinous fragments of life,
Hanging, frowning cliffs, and, all between,
An Ocean of voidness unfathomable.

4
The roaring fires ran o'er the heavens
In whirlwinds and cataracts of blood,
And o'er the dark deserts of Urizen
Fires pour thro' the void, on all sides,
On Urizen's self-begotten armies.

5
But no light from the fires! all was darkness
In the flames of Eternal fury.

6
In fierce anguish and quenchless flames
To the deserts and rocks he ran raging,
To hide; but he could not. Combining,
He dug mountains and hills in vast strength,
He piled them in incessant labour,
In howlings and pangs and fierce madness,
Long periods in burning fires labouring;
Till hoary and age-broke, and aged,
In despair and the shadows of death.

7
And a roof vast, petrific, around
On all sides he framed, like a womb,

Where thousands of rivers, in veins
Of blood, pour down the mountains to cool
The eternal fires, beating without
From Eternals; and like a black Globe,
Viewed by sons of Eternity, standing
On the shore of the infinite ocean,
Like a human heart, struggling and beating,
The vast world of Urizen appeared.

from *The Book of Urizen: Ch 3*

ROBERT BURNS
born 25 January 1759 : died 21 July 1796

Tam o' Shanter

A Tale
'Of brownyis and of bogilis full in this buke.'
Gawin Douglas

When chapman billies leave the street,
And drouthy neebors, neebors meet,
As market-days are wearing late,
An' folk begin to tak' the gate;
While we sit bousing at the nappy,
An' gettin fou and unco happy,
We think na on the lang Scots miles,
The mosses, waters, slaps, and stiles,
That lie between us and our hame,
Where sits our sulky sullen dame,
Gathering her brows like gathering storm,
Nursing her wrath to keep it warm.
This truth fand honest Tam o' Shanter,
As he frae Ayr ae night did canter,
(Auld Ayr, wham ne'er a town surpasses,
For honest men and bonny lasses.)
O Tam! hadst thou but been sae wise,

As ta'en they ain wife Kate's advice!
She tauld thee weel thou was a skellum,
A blethering, blustering, drunken blellum;
That frae November till October,
Ae market-day thou wasna sober;
That ilka melder, wi' the miller,
Thou sat as lang as thou had siller;
That ev'ry naig was ca'd a shoe on,
The smith and thee gat roaring fou on;
That at the Lord's house, ev'n on Sunday,
Thou drank wi' Kirton Jean till Monday.
She prophesy'd, that late or soon,
Thou would be found deep drown'd in Doon;
Or catch'd wi' warlocks in the mirk,
By Alloway's auld haunted kirk.

Ah, gentle dames! it gars me greet,
To think how many counsels sweet,
How mony lengthen'd sage advices,
The husband frae the wife despises!

But to our tale: – Ae market night,
Tam had got planted unco right;
Fast by an ingle bleezing finely,
Wi' reaming swats, that drank divinely;
And at his elbow, Souter Johnny,
His ancient, trusty, drouthy crony;
Tam lo'ed him like a vera brither;
They had been fou' for weeks thegither!
The night drave on wi' sangs an' clatter;
And ay the ale was growing better:
The landlady and Tam grew gracious;
Wi' favours secret, sweet, and precious;
The Souter tauld his queerest stories;
The landlord's laugh was ready chorus:
The storm without might rair and rustle –
Tam did na mind the storm a whistle.

Care, mad to see a man sae happy,
E'en drown'd himself amang the nappy!

As bees flee hame wi' lades o' treasure,
The minutes wing'd their way wi' pleasure:
Kings may be blest, but Tam was glorious,
O'er a' the ills o' life victorious.

But pleasures are like poppies spread,
You seize the flow'r, its bloom is shed;
Or like the snow falls in the river,
A moment white – then melts for ever;
Or like the borealis race,
That flit ere you can point their place;
Or like the rainbow's lovely form
Evanishing amid the storm.
Nae man can tether time or tide;
The hour approaches Tam maun ride;
That hour, o' night's black arch the key-stane,
That dreary hour he mounts his beast in;
And sic a night he taks the road in
As ne'er poor sinner was abroad in.

The wind blew as 'twad blawn its last;
The rattling show'rs rose on the blast;
The speedy gleams the darkness swallow'd;
Loud, deep, and lang the thunder bellow'd:
That night, a child might understand,
The de'il had business on his hand.

Weel mounted on his grey mare, Meg,
A better never lifted leg,
Tam skelpit on thro' dub and mire,
Despising wind, and rain, and fire;
Whiles holding fast his guid blue bonnet;
Whiles crooning o'er some auld Scots sonnet;
Whiles glow'ring round wi' prudent cares,
Lest bogles catch him unawares;
Kirk-Alloway was drawing nigh,
Whare ghaists and houlets nightly cry. –

By this time he was cross the ford,
Whare in the snaw the chapman smoor'd;

And past the birks and meikle stane,
Where drunken Charlie brak's neck-bane;
And thro' the whins, and by the cairn,
Where hunters fand the murder'd bairn;

And near the thorn, aboon the well,
Where Mungo's mither hang'd hersel.
Before him Doon pours all his floods;
The doubling storm roars thro' the woods;
The lightnings flash from pole to pole;
Near and more near the thunders roll;
When, glimmering thro' the groaning trees,
Kirk-Alloway seem'd in a bleeze;
Thro' ilka bore the beams were glancing;
And loud resounded mirth and dancing.

Inspiring bold John Barleycorn!
What dangers thou canst make us scorn!
Wi' tippeny, we fear nae evil;
Wi' usquabae we'll face the devil! –
The swats sae ream'd in Tammie's noddle,
Fair play, he car'd nae deils a boddle.
But Maggie stood right sair astonish'd,
'Till, by the heel and hand admonish'd,
She ventur'd forward on the light;
And wow! Tam saw an unco sight!
Warlocks and witches in a dance;
Nae cotillion brent new frae France,
But hornpipes, jigs, strathspeys, and reels,
Put life and mettle in their heels:
A winnock-bunker in the east,
There sat auld Nick, in shape o' beast;
A towzie tyke, black, grim, and large,
To gie them music was his charge;
He screw'd the pipes and gart them skirl,
Till roof and rafters a' did dirl. –
Coffins stood round, like open presses;
That shaw'd the dead in their last dresses;
And by some devilish cantrip slight
Each in its cauld hand held a light –

By which heroic Tam was able
To note upon the haly table,
A murderer's banes in gibbet airns;
Tw span-lang, wee unchristen'd bairns;
A thief, new-cutted frae a rape,
Wi' his last gasp his gab did gape;
Five tomahawks, wi' bluid red-rusted;
Five scimitars, wi' murder crusted;
A garter, which a babe had strangled;
A knife, a father's throat had mangled,
Whom his ain son o' life bereft,
The gray hairs yet stack to the heft:
Wi' mair o' horrible and awfu',
Which ev'n to name wad be unlawfu'.

As Tammie glowr'd, amaz'd, and curious,
The mirth and fun grew fast and furious:
The piper loud and louder blew;
The dancers quick and quicker flew;
They reel'd, they set, they cross'd, they cleekit,
'Till ilka carlin swat and reekit,
And coost her duddies to the wark,
And linket at it in her sark!

Now Tam, O Tam! had thae been queans
A' plump and strapping, in their teens;
Their sarks instead o' creeshie flannen,
Been snaw-white seventeen hunder linen,
Thir breeks o' mine, my only pair,
That ance were plush, o' guid blue hair,
I wad hae gi'en them off my hurdies,
Far ae blink o' the bonnie burdies!

But wither'd beldams, auld and droll,
Rigwoodie hags, wad spean a foal,
Lowping an' flinging on a cummock,
I wonder didna turn thy stomach.

But Tam kenn'd what was what fu' brawlie,
There was ae winsome wench and walie,

That night enlisted in the core,
(Lang after kenn'd on Carrick shore;
For mony a beast to dead she shot
And perish'd mony a bonnie boat,
And shook baith meikle corn and bear,
And kept the country-side in fear.)

Her cutty sark, o' Paisley harn,
That while a lassie she had worn
In longitude tho' sorely scanty,
It was her best, and she was vauntie –
Ah! little kenn'd thy reverend grannie,
That sark she coft for her wee Nannie,
Wi' twa pund Scots ('twas a' her riches),
Wad ever grac'd a dance of witches!

But here my muse her wing maun cour
Sic flights are far beyond her pow'r;
To sing how Nannie lap and flang,
(A souple jade she was and strang,)
And how Tam stood, like ane bewitch'd,
And thought his very een enrich'd;
Even Satan glowr'd, and fidg'd fu' fain,
And hotch'd and blew wi' might and main:
'Till first ae caper, syne anither,
Tam tint his reason a' thegither,
And roars out, 'Weel done, Cutty-sark!'
And in an instant all was dark:
And scarcely had he Maggie rallied,
When out the hellish legion sallied.

As bees bizz out wi' angry fyke,
When plundering herds assail their byke;
As open pussie's mortal foes,
When, pop! she starts before their nose;
As eager runs the market-crowd,
When 'Catch the thief' resounds aloud;
So Maggie runs, the witches follow,
Wi' mony an eldritch screech and hollow.

Ah, Tam! Ah, Tam! thou'll get thy fairin'!
In hell they'll roast thee like a herrin'!
In vain thy Kate awaits thy comin'!
Kate soon will be a woefu' woman!
Now do thy speedy utmost, Meg,
And win the key-stane of the brig;
There at them thou thy tail may toss,
A running stream they darena cross!
But ere the key-stane she could make,
The fient a tail she had to shake!
For Nannie, far before the rest,
Hard upon noble Maggie prest,
And flew at Tam wi' furious ettle;
But little wist she Maggie's mettle –
Ae spring brought off her master hale,
But left behind her ain gray tail:
The carlin claught her by the rump,
And left poor Maggie scarce a stump.

Now, wha this tale o' truth shall read,
Ilk man and mother's son, take heed:
Whene'er to drink you are inclin'd,
Or cutty-sarks run in your mind,
Think! ye may buy the joys o'er dear –
Remember Tam o' Shanter's mare.

JAMES HOGG

baptized 9 December 1770 : died 21 November 1835

Kilmeny

Bonny Kilmeny gaed up the glen;
But it wasna to meet Duneira's men,
Nor the rosy monk of the isle to see,
For Kilmeny was pure as pure could be.

It was only to hear the yorlin sing,
And pu' the cress-flower round the spring;
The scarlet hypp and the hindberrye,
And the nut that hang frae the hazel tree;
For Kilmeny was pure as pure could be.
But lang may her minny look o'er the wa',
And lang may she seek i' the green-wood shaw;
Lang the laird o' Duneira blame,
And lang, lang greet or Kilmeny come hame!

When many a day had come and fled,
When grief was calm and hope was dead,
When mess for Kilmeny's soul had been sung,
When the bedes-man had prayed, and the dead-bell rung,
Late, late in a gloamin', when all was still,
When the fringe was red on the westlin hill,
The wood was sere, the moon i' the wane,
The reek o' the cot hung over the plain,
Like a little wee cloud in the world its lane;
When the ingle lowed with an eiry leme,
Late, late in the gloamin' Kilmeny came hame!

'Kilmeny, Kilmeny, where have you been?
Lang hae we sought baith holt and den;
By linn, by ford, and green-wood tree,
Yet you are halesome and fair to see.
Where gat you that joup o' the lily scheen?
The bonny snood of the birk sae green?
And these roses, the fairest that ever were seen?
Kilmeny, Kilmeny, where have you been?' –

Kilmeny looked up with a lovely grace,
But nae smile was seen on Kilmeny's face;
As still was her look, and as still was her e'e,
As the stillness that lay on the emerant lea,
Or the mist that sleeps on a waveless sea.
For Kilmeny had been she knew not where,
And Kilmeny had seen what she could not declare;
Kilmeny had been where the cock never crew,
Where the rain never fell, and the wind never blew.

But it seemed as the harp of the sky had rung,
And the airs of heaven played round her tongue,
When she spake of the lovely forms she had seen,
And a land where sin had never been;
A land of love and a land of light,
Withouten sun, or moon, or night;
Where the river swa'd a living stream,
And the light a pure celestial beam;
The land of vision, it would seem,
A still, an everlasting dream.

In yon green-wood there is a waik,
And in that waik there is a wene,
And in that wene there is a maike,
That neither has flesh, blood, nor bane;
And down in yon green-wood he walks his lane.

In that green wene Kilmeny lay,
Her bosom happ'd wi' flowerets gay;
But the air was soft and the silence deep,
And bonny Kilmeny fell sound asleep.
She kenn'd nae mair, nor open'd her e'e,
Till waked by the hymns of a far countrye.

She 'waken'd on couch of the silk sae slim,
All striped wi' the bars of the rainbow's rim;
And lovely beings round were rife,
Who erst had travell'd mortal life;
And aye they smiled and 'gan to speer,
'What spirit has brought this mortal here?'

'Lang have I journey'd the world wide,'
A meek and reverend fere replied;
'Baith night and day I have watch'd the fair,
Eident a thousand years and mair.
Yes, I have watch'd o'er ilk degree,
Wherever blooms femenitye;
But sinless virgin, free of stain
In mind and body, fand I nane.
Never, since the banquet of time,

Found I virgin in her prime,
Till late this bonny maiden I saw
As spotless as the morning snaw:
Full twenty years she has lived as free
As the spirits that sojourn in this countrye.
I have brought her away frae the snares of men,
That sin or death she never may ken.'

They clasp'd her waist and her hands sae fair,
They kiss'd her cheek and they kemed her hair,
And round came many a blooming fere,
Saying, 'Bonny Kilmeny, ye're welcome here!
Women are freed of the littand scorn:
O blest be the day Kilmeny was born!
Now shall the land of the spirits see,
Now shall it ken what a woman may be!
Many a lang year in sorrow and pain,
Many a lang year through the world we've gane,
Commission'd to watch fair womankind,
For it's they who nurice th' immortal mind.
We have watch'd their steps as the dawning shone,
And deep in the green-wood walks alone;
By lily bower and silken bed,
The viewless tears have o'er them shed;
Have soothed their ardent minds to sleep,
Or left the couch of love to weep.
We have seen! we have seen! but the time must come,
And the angels will weep at the day of doom!

'O would the fairest of mortal kind
Aye keep the holy truths in mind,
That kindred spirits their motions see,
Who watch their ways with anxious e'e,
And grieve for the guilt of humanitye!
O, sweet to heaven the maiden's prayer,
And the sigh that heaves a bosom sae fair!
And dear to heaven the words of truth,
And the praise of virtue frae beauty's mouth!
And dear to the viewless forms of air,
The minds that kyth as the body fair!

O bonny Kilmeny! free frae stain,
If ever you seek the world again,
That world of sin, of sorrow and fear,
O tell of the joys that are waiting here!
And tell of the signs you shall shortly see;
Of the times that are now, and the time that shall be.'

They lifted Kilmeny, they led her away,
And she walk'd in the light of a sunless day;
The sky was a dome of crystal bright,
The fountain of vision, and fountain of light:
The emerald fields were of dazzling glow,
And the flowers of everlasting blow.
Then deep in the stream her body they laid,
That her youth and beauty never might fade;
And they smiled on heaven, when they saw her lie
In the stream of life that wander'd bye.
And she heard a song, she heard it sung,
She kend not where; but sae sweetly it rung,
It fell on her ear like a dream of the morn:
'O, blest be the day Kilmeny was born!
Now shall the land of the spirits see,
Now shall it ken what a woman may be!
The sun that shines on the world sae bright,
A borrow'd gleid frae the fountain of light;
And the moon that sleeks the sky sae dun,
Like a gouden bow, or a beamless sun,
Shall wear away, and be seen nae mair,
And the angels shall miss them travelling the air.
But lang, lang after baith night and day,
When the sun and the world have elyed away;
When the sinner has gane to his waesome doom,
Kilmeny shall smile in eternal bloom!'

They bore her away she wist not how,
For she felt not arm nor rest below;
But so swift they wain'd her through the light,
'Twas like the motion of sound or sight;
They seem'd to split the gales of air,
And yet nor gale nor breeze was there.

Unnumber'd groves below them grew,
They came, they pass'd, and backward flew,
Like floods of blossoms gliding on,
In moment seen, in moment gone.
O, never vales to mortal view
Appear'd like those o'er which they flew!
That land to human spirits given,
The lowermost vales of the storied heaven;
From thence they can view the world below,
And heaven's blue gates with sapphires glow,
More glory yet unmeet to know.

They bore her far to a mountain green,
To see what mortal never had seen;
And they seated her high on a purple sward,
And bade her heed what she saw and heard,
And note the changes the spirits wrought,
For now she lived in the land of thought.
She look'd, and she saw nor sun nor skies,
But a crystal dome of a thousand dyes.
She look'd, and she saw nae land aright,
But an endless whirl of glory and light.
And radiant beings went and came,
Far swifter than wind, or the linked flame.
She hid her e'en frae the dazzling view;
She look'd again, and the scene was new.

She saw a sun on a summer sky,
And clouds of amber sailing bye;
A lovely land beneath her lay,
And that land had glens and mountains gray;
And that land had valleys and hoary piles,
And marled seas, and a thousand isles.
Its fields were speckled, its forests green,
And its lakes were all of the dazzling sheen,
Like magic mirrors, where slumbering lay
The sun and the sky and the cloudlet gray;
Which heaved and trembled, and gently swung,
On every shore they seem'd to be hung;
For there they were seen on their downward plain

A thousand times and a thousand again;
In winding lake and placid firth,
Like peaceful heavens in the bosom of earth.

Kilmeny sigh'd and seem'd to grieve,
For she found her hearth to that land did cleave;
She saw the corn wave on the vale,
She saw the deer run down the dale;
She saw the plaid and the broad claymore,
And the brows that the badge of freedom bore;
And she thought she had seen the land before.

She saw a lady sit on a throne,
The fairest that ever the sun shone on!
A lion lick'd her hand of milk,
And she held him in a leish of silk;
And a leifu' maiden stood at her knee,
With a silver wand and melting e'e;
Her sovereign shield till love stole in,
And poison'd all the fount within.

Then a gruff untoward bedesman came,
And hundit the lion on his dame;
And the guardian maid wi' the dauntless e'e,
She dropp'd a tear, and left her knee;
And she saw till the queen frae the lion fled,
Till the bonniest flower of the world lay dead;
A coffin was set on a distant plain,
And she saw the red blood fall like rain;
Then bonny Kilmeny's heart grew sair,
And she turn'd away, and could look nae mair.

Then the gruff grim carle girn'd amain,
And they trampled him down, but he rose again;
And he baited the lion to deeds of weir,
Till he lapp'd the blood to the kingdom dear;
And weening his head was danger-preef,
When crown'd with the rose and clover leaf,
He gowl'd at the carle, and chased him away,
To feed wi' the deer on the mountain gray.

He gowl'd at the carle, and geck'd at Heaven,
But his mark was set, and his arles given.
Kilmeny a while her e'en withdrew;
She look'd again, and the scene was new.

She saw below her fair unfurl'd
One half of all the glowing world,
Where oceans roll'd, and rivers ran,
To bound the aims of sinful man.
She saw a people, fierce and fell,
Burst frae their bounds like fiends of hell;
Their lilies grew, and the eagle flew;
And she herked on her ravening crew,
Till the cities and towers were wrapp'd in a blaze,
And the thunder it roar'd o'er the lands and the seas.
The widows they wail'd, and the red blood ran,
And she threaten'd an end to the race of man;
She never lened, nor stood in awe,
Till caught by the lion's deadly paw.
O, then the eagle swink'd for life,
And brainyell'd up a mortal strife;
But flew she north, or flew she south,
She met wi' the gowl of the lion's mouth.

With a mooted wing and waefu' maen,
The eagle sought her eiry again;
But lang may she cower in her bloody nest,
And lang, lang sleek her wounded breast,
Before she sey another flight,
To play wi' the norland lion's might.

But to sing the sights Kilmeny saw,
So far surpassing nature's law,
The singer's voice wad sink away,
And the string of his harp wad cease to play.
But she saw till the sorrows of man were bye,
And all was love and harmony;
Till the stars of heaven fell calmly away,
Like flakes of snaw on a winter day.

Then Kilmeny begg'd again to see
The friends she had left in her own countrye;
To tell of the place where she had been,
And the glories that lay in the land unseen;
To warn the living maidens fair,
The loved of Heaven, the spirits' care,
That all whose minds unmeled remain
Shall bloom in beauty when time is gane.

With distant music, soft and deep,
They lull'd Kilmeny sound asleep;
And when she awaken'd, she lay her lane,
All happ'd with flowers, in the green-wood wene.
When seven lang years had come and fled,
When grief was calm, and hope was dead;
When scarce was remember'd Kilmeny's name,
Late, late in a gloamin' Kilmeny came hame!

And O, her beauty was fair to see,
But still and steadfast was her e'e!
Such beauty bard may never declare,
For there was no pride nor passion there;
And the soft desire of maiden's e'en
In that mild face could never be seen.
Her seymar was the lily flower,
And her cheek the moss-rose in the shower;
And her voice like the distant melodye,
That floats along the twilight sea.
But she loved to raike the lanely glen,
And keeped afar frae the haunts of men;
Her holy hymns unheard to sing,
To suck the flowers, and drink the spring.
But wherever her peaceful form appear'd,
The wild beasts of the hill were cheer'd;
The wolf play'd blythly round the field,
The lordly byson low'd and kneel'd;
The dun deer woo'd with manner bland,
And cower'd aneath her lily hand.
And when at even the woodlands rung,
When hymns of other worlds she sung

In ecstasy of sweet devotion,
O, then the glen was all in motion!
The wild beasts of the forest came,
Broke from their bughts and faulds the tame,
And goved around, charm'd and amazed;
Even the dull cattle croon'd and gazed,
And murmur'd and look'd with anxious pain
For something the mystery to explain.
The buzzard came with the throstle-cock;
The corby left her houf in the rock;
The blackbird alang wi' the eagle flew;
The hind came tripping o'er the dew;
The wolf and the kid their raike began,
And the tod, and the lamb, and the leveret ran;
The hawk and the hern attour them hung,
And the merle and the mavis forhooy'd their young;
And all in a peaceful ring were hurl'd;
It was like an eve in a sinless world!

When a month and a day had come and gane,
Kilmeny sought the green-wood wene;
There laid her down on the leaves sae green,
And Kilmeny on earth was never mair seen.
But O, the words that fell from her mouth,
Were words of wonder, and words of truth!
But all the land were in fear and dread,
For they kendna whether she was living or dead.
It wasna her hame, and she couldna remain;
She left this world of sorrow and pain,
And return'd to the land of thought again.

from *The Queen's Wake*

SIR WALTER SCOTT
born 15 August 1771 : died 21 September 1832

The Wizard Appears

A secret horror checked the feast,
And chilled the soul of every guest;
Even the high Dame stood half aghast,
She knew some evil on the blast:
The elvish Page fell to the ground,
And, shuddering, muttered, 'Found! found! found!'

Then sudden, through the darkened air
   A flash of lightning came;
So broad, so bright, so red the glare,
   The castle seemed on flame.
Glanced every rafter of the hall,
Glanced every shield upon the wall;
Each trophied beam, each sculptured stone,
Were instant seen, and instant gone;
Full through the guests' bedazzled band
Resistless flashed the levin-brand,
And filled the hall with smouldering smoke,
As on the elvish Page it broke.
   It broke, with thunder long and loud,
   Dismayed the brave, appalled the proud, –
      From sea to sea the larum rung;
   On Berwick wall, and at Carlisle withal,
      To arms the startled warders sprung.
When ended was the dreadful roar,
The elvish Dwarf was seen no more!

Some heard a voice in Branksome Hall,
Some saw a sight, not seen by all;
That dreadful voice was heard by some
Cry, with loud summons, 'Gylbin, come!'
   And on the spot where burst the brand,
      Just where the Page had flung him down,

Some saw an arm, and some a hand,
And some the waving of a gown!
The guests in silence prayed and shook,
And terror dimmed each lofty look.
But none of all the astonished train
Was so dismayed as Deloraine;
His blood did freeze, his brain did burn.
'Twas feared his mind would ne'er return;
For he was speechless, ghastly, wan,
Like him, of whom the story ran,
Who spoke the spectre-hound in Man*.
At length, by fits, he darkly told,
With broken hint, and shuddering cold –
That he had seen, right certainly,
A shape with amice wrapped around,
With a wrought Spanish baldric bound,
Like pilgrim from beyond the sea;
And knew – but how it mattered not –
It was the wizard, Michael Scott!

from *The Lay of the Last Minstrel* : Canto 6

SAMUEL TAYLOR COLERIDGE
born 21 October 1772 : died 25 July 1834

Christabel

Part 1
'Tis the middle of night by the castle clock,
And the owls have awakened the crowing cock;
Tu – whit! – – – Tu – whoo!
And hark, again! the crowing cock,
How drowsily it crew.
Sir Leoline, the Baron rich,
Hath a toothless mastiff bitch;

* The Isle of Man.

From her kennel beneath the rock
She maketh answer to the clock,
Four for the quarters, and twelve for the hour;
Ever and aye, by shine and shower,
Sixteen short howls, not over loud;
Some say, she sees my lady's shroud.

Is the night chilly and dark?
The night is chilly, but not dark.
The thin grey cloud is spread on high,
It covers but not hides the sky.
The moon is behind, and at the full;
And yet she looks both small and dull.
The night is chill, the cloud is grey:
'Tis a month before the month of May,
And the Spring comes slowly up this way.

The lovely lady, Christabel,
Whom her father loves so well,
What makes her in the wood so late,
A furlong from the castle gate?
She had dreams all yesternight
Of her own betrothéd knight;
And she in the midnight wood will pray
For the weal of her lover that's far away.

She stole along, she nothing spoke,
The sighs she heaved were soft and low,
And naught was green upon the oak
But moss and rarest mistletoe:
She kneels beneath the huge oak tree,
And in silence prayeth she.

The lady sprang up suddenly,
The lovely lady, Christabel!
It moaned as near, as near can be,
But what it is she cannot tell. –
On the other side it seems to be,
Of the huge, broad-breasted, old oak tree.

The night is chill; the forest bare;
Is it the wind that moaneth bleak?
There is not wind enough in the air
To move away the ringlet curl
From the lovely lady's cheek –
There is not wind enough to twirl
The one red leaf, the last of its clan,
That dances as often as dance it can,
Hanging so light, and hanging so high,
On the topmost twig that looks up at the sky.

Hush, beating heart of Christabel!
Jesu, Maria, shield her well!
She folded her arms beneath her cloak,
And stole to the other side of the oak.
  What sees she there?

There she sees a damsel bright,
Drest in a silken robe of white,
That shadowy in the moonlight shone:
The neck that made that white robe wan,
Her stately neck, and arms were bare;
Her blue-veined feet unsandal'd were,
And wildly glittered here and there
The gems entangled in her hair.
I guess, 'twas frightful there to see
A lady so richly clad as she –
Beautiful exceedingly!

Mary mother, save me now!
(Said Christabel,) And who art thou?

The lady strange made answer meet,
And her voice was faint and sweet: –
Have pity on my sore distress,
I scarce can speak for weariness:
Stretch forth thy hand, and have no fear!
Said Christabel, How camest thou here?
And the lady, whose voice was faint and sweet,
Did thus pursue her answer meet: –

My sire is of a noble line,
And my name is Geraldine:
Five warriors seized me yestermorn,
Me, even me, a maid forlorn:
They choked my cries with force and fright,
And tied me on a palfrey white.
The palfrey was as fleet as wind,
And they rode furiously behind.
They spurred amain, their steeds were white:
And once we crossed the shade of night.
As sure as Heaven shall rescue me,
I have no thought what men they be;
Nor do I know how long it is
(For I have lain entranced I wis)
Since one, the tallest of the five,
Took me from the palfrey's back,
A weary woman, scarce alive.
Some muttered words his comrades spoke:
He placed me underneath this oak:
He swore they would return with haste;
Whither they went I cannot tell –
I thought I heard, some minutes past,
Sounds as of a castle bell.
Stretch forth thy hand (thus ended she),
And help a wretched maid to flee.

Then Christabel stretched forth her hand,
And comforted fair Geraldine:
O well, bright dame! may you command
The service of Sir Leoline;
And gladly our stout chivalry
Will he send forth and friends withal
To guide and guard you safe and free
Home to your noble father's hall.

She rose: and forth with steps they passed
That strove to be, and were not, fast.
Her gracious stars the lady blest,
And thus spake on sweet Christabel:
All our household are at rest,

The hall as silent as the cell;
Sir Leoline is weak in health,
And may not well awakened be,
But we will move as if in stealth,
And I beseech your courtesy,
This night, to share your couch with me.

They crossed the moat, and Christabel
Took the key that fitted well;
A little door she opened straight,
All in the middle of the gate;
The gate that was ironed within and without,
Where an army in battle array had marched out.
The lady sank, belike through pain,
And Christabel with might and main
Lifted her up, a weary weight,
Over the threshold of the gate:
Then the lady rose again,
And moved, as she were not in pain.

So free from danger, free from fear,
They crossed the court: right glad they were.
And Christabel devoutly cried
To the lady by her side,
Praise we the Virgin all divine
Who hath rescued thee from thy distress!
Alas, alas! said Geraldine,
I cannot speak for weariness.
So free from danger, free from fear,
They crossed the court: right glad they were.

Outside her kennel, the mastiff old
Lay fast asleep, in moonshine cold.
The mastiff old did not awake,
Yet she an angry moan did make!
And what can ail the mastiff bitch?
Never till now she uttered yell
Beneath the eye of Christabel.
Perhaps it is the owlet's scritch:
For what can ail the mastiff bitch?

They passed the hall, that echoes still,
Pass as lightly as you will!
The brands were flat, the brands were dying,
Amid their own white ashes lying;
But when the lady passed, there came
A tongue of light, a fit of flame;
And Christabel saw the lady's eye,
And nothing else saw she thereby,
Save the boss of the shield of Sir Leoline tall,
Which hung in a murky old niche in the wall.
O softly tread, said Christabel,
My father seldom sleepeth well.

Sweet Christabel her feet doth bare,
And jealous of the listening air
They steal their way from stair to stair,
Now in glimmer, and now in gloom,
And now they pass the Baron's room,
As still as death, with stifled breath!
And now have reached her chamber door;
And now doth Geraldine press down
The rushes of the chamber floor.

The moon shines dim in the open air,
And not a moonbeam enters here.
But they without its light can see
The chamber carved so curiously,
Carved with figures strange and sweet,
All made out of the carver's brain,
For a lady's chamber meet:
The lamp with twofold silver chain
Is fastened to an angel's feet.

The silver lamp burns dead and dim;
But Christabel the lamp will trim.
She trimmed the lamp, and made it bright,
And left it swinging to and fro,
While Geraldine, in wretched plight,
Sank down upon the floor below.

O weary lady, Geraldine,
I pray you, drink this cordial wine!
It is a wine of virtuous powers;
My mother made it of wild flowers.

And will your mother pity me,
Who am a maiden most forlorn?
Christabel answered – Woe is me!
She died the hour that I was born.
I have heard the grey-haired friar tell
How on her death-bed she did say,
That she should hear the castle-bell
Strike twelve upon my wedding-day.
O mother dear! that thou wert here!
I would, said Geraldine, she were!

But soon with altered voice, said she –
'Off, wandering mother! Peak and pine!
I have power to bid thee flee.'
Alas! what ails poor Geraldine?
Why stares she with unsettled eye?
Can she the bodiless dead espy?
And why with hollow voice cries she,
'Off, woman, off! this hour is mine –
Though thou her guardian spirit be,
Off, woman, off! 'tis given to me.'

Then Christabel knelt by the lady's side,
And raised to heaven her eyes so blue –
Alas! said she, this ghastly ride –
Dear lady! it hath wildered you!
The lady wiped her moist cold brow,
And faintly said, ' 'tis over now!'

Again the wild-flower wine she drank:
Her fair large eyes 'gan glitter bright,
And from the floor whereon she sank,
The lofty lady stood upright:
She was most beautiful to see,
Like a lady of a far countrée.

And thus the lofty lady spake –
'All they who live in the upper sky,
Do love you, holy Christabel!
And you love them, and for their sake
And for the good which me befel,
Even I in my degree will try,
Fair maiden, to requite you well.
But now unrobe yourself; for I
Must pray, ere yet in bed I lie.'

Quoth Christabel, So let it be!
And as the lady bade, did she.
Her gentle limbs did she undress,
And lay down in her loveliness.

But through her brain of weal and woe
So many thoughts moved to and fro,
That vain it were her lids to close;
So half-way from the bed she rose,
And on her elbow did recline
To look at the lady Geraldine.

Beneath the lamp the lady bowed,
And slowly rolled her eyes around;
Then drawing in her breath aloud,
Like one that shuddered, she unbound
The cincture from beneath her breast:
Her silken robe, and inner vest,
Dropt to her feet, and full in view,
Behold! her bosom and half her side –
A sight to dream of, not to tell!
O shield her! shield sweet Christabel!

Yet Geraldine nor speaks nor stirs;
Ah! what a stricken look was hers!
Deep from within she seems half-way
To lift some weight with sick assay,
And eyes the maid and seeks delay;
Then suddenly, as one defied,
Collects herself in scorn and pride,

And lay down by the Maiden's side! –
And in her arms the maid she took,
Ah wel-a-day!
And with low voice and doleful look
These words did say:
'In the touch of this bosom there worketh a spell,
Which is lord of thy utterance, Christabel!
Thou knowest to-night, and wilt know to-morrow,
This mark of my shame, this seal of my sorrow;
But vainly thou warrest,
For this is alone in
Thy power to declare,
That in the dim forest
Thou heard'st a low moaning,
And found'st a bright lady, surpassingly fair;
And didst bring her home with thee in love and in charity,
To shield her and shelter her from the damp air.'

The Conclusion to Part 1

It was a lovely sight to see
The lady Christabel, when she
Was praying at the old oak tree.
Amid the jaggéd shadows
Of mossy leafless boughs,
Kneeling in the moonlight,
To make her gentle vows;
Her slender palms together prest,
Heaving sometimes on her breast;
Her face resigned to bliss or bale –
Her face, oh call it fair not pale,
And both blue eyes more bright than clear,
Each about to have a tear.

With open eyes (ah woe is me!)
Asleep, and dreaming fearfully,
Fearfully dreaming, yet, I wis,
Dreaming that alone, which is –
O sorrow and shame! Can this be she,
The lady, who knelt at the old oak tree?

And lo! the worker of these harms,
That holds the maiden in her arms,
Seems to slumber still and mild,
As a mother with her child.

A star hath set, a star hath risen,
O Geraldine! since arms of thine
Have been the lovely lady's prison.
O Geraldine! one hour was thine –
Thou'st had thy will! By tairn and rill,
The night-birds all that hour were still.
But now they are jubilant anew,
From cliff and tower, tu – whoo! tu – whoo!
Tu – whoo! tu – whoo! from wood and fell!

And see! the lady Christabel
Gathers herself from out her trance;
Her limbs relax, her countenance
Grows sad and soft; the smooth thin lids
Close o'er her eyes; and tears she sheds –
Large tears that leave the lashes bright!
And oft the while she seems to smile
As infants at a sudden light!

Yea, she doth smile, and she doth weep,
Like a youthful hermitess,
Beauteous in a wilderness,
Who, praying always, prays in sleep.
And, if she move unquietly,
Perchance, 'tis but the blood so free
Comes back and tingles in her feet.
No doubt, she hath a vision sweet.
What if her guardian spirit 'twere,
What if she knew her mother near?
But this she knows, in joys and woes,
That saints will aid if men will call:
For the blue sky bends over all!

Part 2

Each matin bell, the Baron saith,
Knells us back to a world of death.
These words Sir Leoline first said,
When he rose and found his lady dead:
These words Sir Leoline will say
Many a morn to his dying day!

And hence the custom and law began
That still at dawn the sacristan,
Who duly pulls the heavy bell,
Five and forty beads must tell
Between each stroke – a warning knell,
Which not a soul can choose but hear
From Bratha Head to Wyndermere.

Saith Bracy the bard, So let it knell!
And let the drowsy sacristan
Still count as slowly as he can!
There is no lack of such, I ween,
As well fill up the space between.
In Langdale Pike and Witch's Lair,
And Dungeon-ghyll so foully rent,
With ropes of rock and bells of air
Three sinful sextons' ghosts are pent,
Who all give back, one after t'other,
The death-note to their living brother;
And oft too, by the knell offended,
Just as their one! two! three! is ended,
The devil mocks the doleful tale
With a merry peal from Borodale.

The air is still! through mist and cloud
That merry peal comes ringing loud;
And Geraldine shakes off her dread,
And rises lightly from the bed;
Puts on her silken vestments white,
And tricks her hair in lovely plight,
And nothing doubting of her spell

Awakens the lady Christabel.
'Sleep you, sweet lady Christabel?
I trust that you have rested well.'

And Christabel awoke and spied
The same who lay down by her side –
O rather say, the same whom she
Raised up beneath the old oak tree!
Nay, fairer yet! and yet more fair!
For she belike hath drunken deep
Of all the blessedness of sleep!
And while she spake, her looks, her air
Such gentle thankfulness declare,
That (so it seemed) her girded vests
Grew tight beneath her heaving breasts.
'Sure I have sinn'd!' said Christabel,
'Now heaven be praised if all be well!'
And in low faltering tones, yet sweet,
Did she the lofty lady greet
With such perplexity of mind
As dreams too lively leave behind.

So quickly she rose, and quickly arrayed
Her maiden limbs, and having prayed
That He, who on the cross did groan,
Might wash away her sins unknown,
So forthwith led fair Geraldine
To meet her sire, Sir Leoline.

The lovely maid and the lady tall
Are pacing both into the hall,
And pacing on through page and groom,
Enter the Baron's presence-room.

The Baron rose, and while he prest
His gentle daughter to his breast,
With cheerful wonder in his eyes
The lady Geraldine espies,
And gave such welcome to the same,
As might beseem so bright a dame!

But when he heard the lady's tale,
And when she told her father's name,
Why waxed Sir Leoline so pale,
Murmuring o'er the name again,
Lord Roland de Vaux of Tryermaine?

Alas! they had been friends in youth;
But whispering tongues can poison truth;
And constancy lives in realms above;
And life is thorny; and youth is vain;
And to be wroth with one we love
Doth work like madness in the brain.
And thus it chanced, as I divine,
With Roland and Sir Leoline.
Each spake words of high disdain
And insult to his heart's best brother:
They parted – ne'er to meet again!
But never either found another
To free the hollow heart from paining –
They stood aloof, the scars remaining,
Like cliffs which had been rent asunder;
A dreary sea now flows between; –
But neither heat, nor frost, nor thunder,
Shall wholly do away, I ween,
The marks of that which once hath been.

Sir Leoline, a moment's space,
Stood gazing on the damsel's face:
And the youthful Lord of Tryermaine
Came back upon his heart again.

O then the Baron forgot his age,
His noble heart swelled high with rage;
He swore by the wounds in Jesu's side
He would proclaim it far and wide,
With trump and solemn heraldry,
That they, who thus had wronged the dame,
Were base as spotted infamy!
'And if they dare deny the same,
My herald shall appoint a week,

And let the recreant traitors seek
My tourney court – that there and then
I may dislodge their reptile souls
From the bodies and forms of men!'
He spake: his eye in lightning rolls!
For the lady was ruthlessly seized; and he kenned
In the beautiful lady the child of his friend!

And now the tears were on his face,
And fondly in his arms he took
Fair Geraldine, who met the embrace,
Prolonging it with joyous look.
Which when she viewed, a vision fell
Upon the soul of Christabel,
The vision of fear, the touch and pain!
She shrunk and shuddered, and saw again –
(Ah, woe is me! Was it for thee,
Thou gentle maid! such sights to see?)

Again she saw that bosom old,
Again she felt that bosom cold,
And drew in her breath with a hissing sound:
Whereat the Knight turned wildly round,
And nothing saw, but his own sweet maid
With eyes upraised, as one that prayed.

The touch, the sight, had passed away,
And in its stead that vision blest,
Which comforted her after-rest
While in the lady's arms she lay,
Had put a rapture in her breast,
And on her lips and o'er her eyes
Spread smiles like light!
With new surprise,
'What ails then my belovéd child?'
The Baron said – His daughter mild
Made answer, 'All will yet be well!'
I ween, she had no power to tell
Aught else: so mighty was the spell.

Yet he, who saw this Geraldine,
Had deemed her sure a thing divine:
Such sorrow with such grace she blended,
As if she feared she had offended
Sweet Christabel, that gentle maid!
And with such lowly tones she prayed
She might be sent without delay
Home to her father's mansion.
'Nay!
Nay, by my soul!' said Leoline.
'Ho! Bracy the bard, the charge be thine!
Go thou, with music sweet and loud,
And take two steeds with trappings proud,
And take the youth whom thou lov'st best
To bear thy harp, and learn thy song,
And clothe you both in solemn vest,
And over the mountains haste along,
Lest wandering folk, that are abroad,
Detain you on the valley road.

'And when he has crossed the Irthing flood,
My merry bard! he hastes, he hastes
Up Knorren Moor, through Halegarth Wood,
And reaches soon that castle good
Which stands and threatens Scotland's wastes.

'Bard Bracy! bard Bracy! your horses are fleet,
Ye must ride up the hall, your music so sweet,
More loud than your horses' echoing feet!
And loud and loud to Lord Roland call,
Thy daughter is safe in Langdale hall!
Thy beautiful daughter is safe and free –
Sir Leoline greets thee thus through me!
He bids thee come without delay
With all thy numerous array
And take thy lovely daughter home:
And he will meet thee on the way
With all his numerous array
White with their panting palfreys' foam:
And, by mine honour! I will say,

That I repent me of the day
When I spake words of fierce disdain
To Roland de Vaux of Tryermaine! –
– For since that evil hour hath flown,
Many a summer's sun hath shone;
Yet ne'er found I a friend again
Like Roland de Vaux of Tryermaine.'

The lady fell, and clasped his knees,
Her face upraised, her eyes o'erflowing;
And Bracy replied, with faltering voice,
His gracious Hail on all bestowing! –
'Thy words, thou sire of Christabel,
Are sweeter than my harp can tell;
Yet might I gain a boon of thee,
This day my journey should not be,
So strange a dream hath come to me,
That I had vowed with music loud
To clear yon wood from thing unblest,
Warned by a vision in my rest!
For in my sleep I saw that dove,
That gentle bird, whom thou dost love,
And call'st by thy own daughter's name –
Sir Leoline! I saw the same
Fluttering, and uttering fearful moan,
Among the green herbs in the forest alone.
Which when I saw and when I heard,
I wonder'd what might ail the bird;
For nothing near it could I see,
Save the grass and green herbs underneath the old tree.

'And in my dream methought I went
To search out what might there be found;
And what the sweet bird's trouble meant,
That thus lay fluttering on the ground.
I went and peered, and could descry
No cause for her distressful cry;
But yet for her dear lady's sake
I stooped, methought, the dove to take,
When lo! I saw a bright green snake

Coiled around its wings and neck.
Green as the herbs on which it couched,
Close by the dove's its head it crouched;
And with the dove it heaves and stirs,
Swelling its neck as she swelled hers!
I woke; it was the midnight hour,
The clock was echoing in the tower;
But though my slumber was gone by,
This dream it would not pass away –
It seems to live upon my eye!
And thence I vowed this self-same day
With music strong and saintly song
To wander through the forest bare,
Lest aught unholy loiter there.'

Thus Bracy said: the Baron, the while,
Half-listening heard him with a smile;
Then turned to Lady Geraldine,
His eyes made up of wonder and love;
And said in courtly accents fine,
'Sweet maid, Lord Roland's beauteous dove,
With arms more strong than harp or song,
Thy sire and I will crush the snake!'
He kissed her forehead as he spake,
And Geraldine in maiden wise
Casting down her large bright eyes,
With blushing cheek and courtesy fine
She turned her from Sir Leoline;
Softly gathering up her train,
That o'er her right arm fell again;
And folded her arms across her chest,
And couched her head upon her breast,
And looked askance at Christabel –
Jesu, Maria, shield her well!

A snake's small eye blinks dull and shy;
And the lady's eyes they shrunk in her head,
Each shrunk up to a serpent's eye,
And with somewhat of malice, and more of dread,
At Christabel she looked askance! –

One moment – and the sight was fled!
But Christabel in dizzy trance
Stumbling on the unsteady ground
Shuddered aloud, with a hissing sound;
And Geraldine again turned round,
And like a thing, that sought relief,
Full of wonder and full of grief,
She rolled her large bright eyes divine
Wildly on Sir Leoline.

The maid, alas! her thoughts are gone,
She nothing sees – no sight but one!
The maid, devoid of guile and sin,
I know not how, in fearful wise,
So deeply had she drunken in
That look, those shrunken serpent eyes,
That all her features were resigned
To this sole image in her mind:
And passively did imitate
That look of dull and treacherous hate!
And thus she stood, in dizzy trance,
Still picturing that look askance
With forced unconscious sympathy
Full before her father's view –
As far as such a look could be
In eyes so innocent and blue!

And when the trance was o'er, the maid
Paused awhile, and inly prayed:
Then falling at the Baron's feet,
'By my mother's soul do I entreat
That thou this woman send away!'
She said: and more she could not say:
For what she knew she could not tell,
O'er-mastered by the mighty spell.

Why is thy cheek so wan and wild,
Sir Leoline? Thy only child
Lies at thy feet, thy joy, thy pride,
So fair, so innocent, so mild;

The same, for whom thy lady died!
O by the pangs of her dear mother
Think thou no evil of thy child!
For her, and thee, and for no other,
She prayed the moment ere she died:
Prayed that the babe for whom she died,
Might prove her dear lord's joy and pride!
   That prayer her deadly pangs beguiled,
         Sir Leoline!
   And wouldst thou wrong thy only child,
         Her child and thine?

Within the Baron's heart and brain
If thoughts, like these, had any share,
They only swelled his rage and pain,
And did but work confusion there.
His heart was cleft with pain and rage,
His cheeks they quivered, his eyes were wild,
Dishonoured thus in his old age;
Dishonoured by his only child,
And all his hospitality
To the wronged daughter of his friend
By more than woman's jealousy
Brought thus to a disgraceful end –
He rolled his eye with stern regard
Upon the gentle minstrel bard,
And said in tones abrupt, austere –
'Why, Bracy! dost thou loiter here?
I bade thee hence!' The bard obeyed;
And turning from his own sweet maid,
The agéd knight, Sir Leoline,
Led forth the lady Geraldine!

The Conclusion to Part 2

A little child, a limber elf,
Singing, dancing to itself,
A fairy thing with red round cheeks,
That always finds, and never seeks,
Makes such a vision to the sight

As fills a father's eyes with light;
And pleasures flow in so thick and fast
Upon his heart, that he at last
Must needs express his love's excess
With words of unmeant bitterness.
Perhaps 'tis pretty to force together
Thoughts so all unlike each other;
To mutter and mock a broken charm,
To dally with wrong that does no harm.
Perhaps 'tis tender too and pretty
At each wild word to feel within
A sweet recoil of love and pity.
And what, if in a world of sin
(O sorrow and shame should this be true!)
Such giddiness of heart and brain
Comes seldom save from rage and pain,
So talks as it's most used to do.

Kubla Khan

In Xanadu did Kubla Khan
A stately pleasure-dome decree:
Where Alph, the sacred river, ran
Through caverns measureless to man
   Down to a sunless sea.
So twice five miles of fertile ground
With walls and towers were girdled round:
And there were gardens bright with sinuous rills,
Where blossomed many an incense-bearing tree;
And here were forests ancient as the hills,
Enfolding sunny spots of greenery.

But oh! that deep romantic chasm which slanted
Down the green hill athwart a cedarn cover!
A savage place! as holy and enchanted
As e'er beneath a waning moon was haunted
By woman wailing for her demon-lover!

And from this chasm, with ceaseless turmoil seething,
As if this earth in fast thick pants were breathing,
A mighty fountain momently was forced:
Amid whose swift half-intermitted burst
Huge fragments vaulted like rebounding hail,
Or chaffy grain beneath the thresher's flail:
And 'mid these dancing rocks at once and ever
It flung up momently the sacred river.
Five miles meandering with a mazy motion
Through wood and dale the sacred river ran,
Then reached the caverns measureless to man,
And sank in tumult to a lifeless ocean:
And 'mid this tumult Kubla heard from far
Ancestral voices prophesying war!
  The shadow of the dome of pleasure
  Floated midway on the waves;
  Where was heard the mingled measure
  From the fountain and the caves.
It was a miracle of rare device,
A sunny pleasure-dome with caves of ice!

  A damsel with a dulcimer
  In a vision once I saw:
  It was an Abyssinian maid,
  And on her dulcimer she played,
  Singing of Mount Abora.
  Could I revive within me
  Her symphony and song,
  To such a deep delight 'twould win me,
That with music loud and long,
I would build that dome in air,
That sunny dome! those caves of ice!
And all who heard should see them there,
And all should cry, Beware! Beware!
His flashing eyes, his floating hair!
Weave a circle round him thrice,
And close your eyes with holy dread,
For he on honey-dew hath fed,
And drunk the milk of Paradise.

The Rime of the Ancient Mariner

Part 1

An ancient Mariner meeteth three gallants bidden to a wedding feast, and detaineth one.

It is an ancient Mariner,
And he stoppeth one of three.
'By the long grey beard and glittering eye,
Now wherefore stopp'st thou me?

The Bridegroom's doors are opened wide,
And I am next of kin;
The guests are met, the feast is set:
May'st hear the merry din.'

He holds him with his skinny hand,
'There was a ship,' quoth he.
'Hold off! unhand me, greybeard loon!'
Eftsoons his hand dropt he.

The Wedding Guest is spell-bound by the eye of the old seafaring man and constrained to hear his tale.

He holds him with his glittering eye –
The Wedding-Guest stood still,
And listens like a three years' child:
The Mariner hath his will.

The Wedding-Guest sat on a stone:
He cannot choose but hear;
And thus spake on that ancient man,
The bright-eyed Mariner.

'The ship was cheered, the harbour cleared,
Merrily did we drop
Below the kirk, below the hill,
Below the lighthouse top.

The Mariner tells how the ship sailed southward with a good wind and fair weather, till it reached the Line.

'The Sun came up upon the left,
Out of the sea came he!
And he shone bright, and on the right
Went down into the sea.

'Higher and higher every day,
Till over the mast at noon ...'
The Wedding-Guest here beat his breast,
For he heard the loud bassoon.

The bride hath paced into the hall,
Red as a rose is she;
Nodding their heads before her goes
The merry minstrelsy.

The Wedding-Guest heareth the bridal music; but the Mariner continueth his tale.

The Wedding-Guest he beat his breast,
Yet he cannot choose but hear;
And thus spake on that ancient man,
The bright-eyed Mariner.

'And now the storm-blast came, and he
Was tyrannous and strong:
He struck with his o'ertaking wings,
And chased us south along.

The ship driven by a storm toward the South Pole.

'With sloping masts and dipping prow,
As who pursued with yell and blow
Still treads the shadow of his foe
And forward bends his head,
The ship drove fast, loud roared the blast,
And southward aye we fled.

'And now there came both mist and snow
And it grew wondrous cold:
And ice, mast-high, came floating by,
As green as emerald.

'And through the drifts the snowy clifts
Did send a dismal sheen:
Nor shapes of men nor beasts we ken –
The ice was all between.

The land of ice, and of fearful sounds, where no living thing was to be seen.

'The ice was here, the ice was there,
The ice was all around:
It cracked and growled, and roared and howled,

Like noises in a swound!

Till a great sea-bird, called the Albatross, came through the snow-fog and was received with great joy and hospitality.

'At length did cross an Albatross:
Through the fog it came;
As if it had been a Christian soul,
We hailed it in God's name.

'It ate the food it ne'er had eat,
And round and round it flew.
The ice did split with a thunder-fit;
The helmsman steered us through!

And lo! the Albatross proveth a bird of good omen, and followeth the ship as it returned northward through fog and floating ice.

'And a good south wind sprung up behind;
The Albatross did follow,
And every day, for food or play,
Came to the mariner's hollo!

'In mist or cloud, on mast or shroud,
It perched for vespers nine;
Whiles all the night, through fog-smoke white,
Glimmered the white moonshine.'

The ancient Mariner inhospitably killeth the pious bird of good omen.

'God save thee, ancient Mariner!
From the fiends that plague thee thus! –
Why look'st thou so?' – 'With my cross-bow
I shot the Albatross.

Part 2

'The Sun now rose upon the right:
Out of the sea came he,
Still hid in mist, and on the left
Went down into the sea.

'And the good south wind still blew behind,
But no sweet bird did follow,
Nor any day for food or play
Came to the mariner's hollo!

His ship-mates

'And I had done a hellish thing,

And it would work 'em woe:
For all averred, I had killed the bird
That made the breeze to blow.
Ah wretch! said they, the bird to slay,
That made the breeze to blow!

cry out against the ancient Mariner for killing the bird of good luck.

'Nor dim nor red, like God's own head,
The glorious Sun uprist:
Then all averred, I had killed the bird
That brought the fog and mist.
'Twas right, said they, such birds to slay,
That bring the fog and mist.

But when the fog cleared off, they justify the same, and thus make themselves accomplices in the crime.

'The fair breeze blew, the white foam flew,
The furrow followed free;
We were the first that ever burst
Into that silent sea.

The fair breeze continues; the ship enters the Pacific Ocean, & sails northward, even till it reaches the Line.

'Down dropt the breeze, the sails dropt down,
'Twas sad as sad could be;
And we did speak only to break
The silence of the sea!

The ship hath been suddenly becalmed.

'All in a hot and copper sky,
The bloody Sun, at noon,
Right up above the mast did stand,
No bigger than the moon.

'Day after day, day after day,
We stuck, nor breath nor motion;
As idle as a painted ship
Upon a painted ocean.

'Water, water, everywhere,
And all the boards did shrink;
Water, water, everywhere,
Nor any drop to drink.

And the Albatross begins to be avenged.

'The very deep did rot: O Christ!
That ever this should be!

A Spirit had followed them, one of the invisible inhabitants of this planet, neither departed soul nor angels; concerning whom the learned Jew, Josephus, and the Platonic Constantinopolitan, Michael Psellus, may be consulted. They are very numerous, and there is no climate or element without one or more.

Yea, slimy things did crawl with legs
Upon the slimy sea.

'About, about, in reel and rout
The death-fires danced at night;
The water, like a witch's oils,
Burnt green, and blue and white.

'And some in dreams assurèd were
Of the spirit that plagued us so;
Nine fathom deep he had followed us
From the land of mist and snow.

'And every tongue, through utter drought,
Was withered at the root;
We could not speak, no more than if
We had been choked with soot.

The ship-mates in their sore distress, would faint throw the whole guilt on the ancient Mariner: in sign whereof they hang the dead sea-bird round his neck.

'Ah! well-a-day! what evil looks
Had I from old and young!
Instead of the cross, the Albatross
About my neck was hung.

Part 3

'There passed a weary time. Each throat
Was parched, and glazed each eye.
A weary time! a weary time!
How glazed each weary eye,
When looking westward, I beheld
A something in the sky.

The ancient Mariner beholdeth a sign in the element afar off.

'At first it seemed a little speck,
And then it seemed a mist;
It moved and moved, and took at last
A certain shape, I wist.

'A speck, a mist, a shape, I wist!
And still it neared and neared:
As if it dodged a watersprite,

It plunged and tacked and veered.

'With throats unslaked, with black lips baked,
We could nor laugh nor wail;
Through utter drought all dumb we stood!
I bit my arm, I sucked the blood,
And cried, A sail! a sail!

At its nearer approach, it seemeth him to be a ship; and at a dear ransom be freeth his speech from the bonds of thirst.

'With throats unslaked, with black lips baked,
Agape they heard me call:
Gramercy! they for joy did grin,
And all at once their breath drew in,
As they were drinking all.

A flash of joy;

'See! see! (I cried) she tacks no more!
Hither to work us weal;
Without a breeze, without a tide,
She steadies with upright keel!

And horror follows. For can it be a ship that comes onward without wind or tide?

'The western wave was all a-flame.
The day was well-nigh done!
Almost upon the western wave
Rested the broad bright Sun;
When that strange shape drove suddenly
Betwixt us and the Sun.

'And straight the Sun was flecked with bars,
(Heaven's Mother send us grace!)
As if through a dungeon-grate he peered
With broad and burning face.

It seemeth him but the skeleton of a ship.

'Alas! (thought I, and my heart beat loud)
How fast she nears and nears!
Are those *her* sails that glance in the Sun,
Like restless gossameres?

And its ribs are seen as bars on the face of the setting Sun.

'Are those *her* ribs through which the Sun
Did peer, as through a grate?
And is that Woman all her crew?
Is that a Death? and are there two?

The Spectre-Woman and her Death-mate, and no other,

on board the skeleton ship. Like vessel like crew! Death and Life-in-Death have diced for the ship's crew, and she (the latter) winneth the ancient Mariner.

Is Death that woman's mate?

'*Her* lips were red, *her* looks were free,
Her locks were yellow as gold:
Her skin was as white as leprosy,
The Night-mare Life-in-Death was she,
Who thicks man's blood with cold.

'The naked hulk alongside came
And the twain were casting dice;
"The game is done! I've won, I've won!"
Quoth she, and whistles thrice.

No twilight within the courts of the Sun.

'The Sun's rim dips; the stars rush out:
At one stride comes the dark;
With far-heard whisper, o'er the sea,
Off shot the spectre-bark.

At the rising of the Moon.

'We listened and looked sideways up!
Fear at my heart, as at a cup,
My life-blood seemed to sip!
The stars were dim, and thick the night,
The steersman's face by his lamp gleamed white;
From the sails the dew did drip –
Till clomb above the eastern bar
The hornèd moon, with one bright star
Within the nether tip.

One after another.

'One after one, by the star-dogged Moon,
Too quick for groan or sigh,
Each turned his face with a ghastly pang,
And cursed me with his eye.

His shipmates drop down dead.

'Four times fifty living men,
(And I heard nor sigh nor groan)
With heavy thump, a lifeless lump,
They dropped down one by one.

But Life-in-Death begins

'The souls did from their bodies fly, –
They fled to bliss or woe!

And every soul, it passed me by,
Like the whizz of my cross-bow!'

her work on the ancient Mariner.

Part 4

'I fear thee, ancient Mariner!
I fear thy skinny hand!
And thou art long, and lank, and brown,
As is the ribbed sea-sand.

The Wedding-Guest feareth that a Spirit is talking to him;

'I fear thee and thy glittering eye,
And thy skinny hand, so brown.' –
'Fear not, fear not, thou Wedding-Guest!
This body dropt not down.

But the ancient Mariner assureth him of his bodily life, and proceedeth to relate his horrible penance.

'Alone, alone, all, all alone,
Alone on a wide wide sea!
And never a saint took pity on
My soul in agony.

'The many men, so beautiful!
And they all dead did lie:
And a thousand thousand slimy things
Lived on; and so did I.

He despiseth the creatures of the calm.

'I looked upon the rotting sea,
And drew my eyes away;
I looked upon the rotting deck,
And there the dead men lay.

And envieth that they should live, and so many lie dead.

'I looked to Heaven, and tried to pray;
But or ever a prayer had gusht,
A wicked whisper came, and made
My heart as dry as dust.

'I closed my lids, and kept them close,
And the balls like pulses beat;
For the sky and the sea, and the sea and the sky
Lay like a load on my weary eye,
And the dead were at my feet.

But the curse liveth for him in the eye of the dead men.

'The cold sweat melted from their limbs,
Nor rot nor reek did they;
The look with which they looked on me
Had never passed away.

In his loneliness and fixedness he yearneth towards the journeying Moon, and the stars that still sojourn, yet still move onward; and everywhere the blue sky belongs to them, and is their appointed rest and their native country and their own natural homes, which they enter unannounced, as lords that are certainly expected, and yet there is a silent joy at their arrival.

'An orphan's curse would drag to hell
A spirit from on high;
But oh! more horrible than that
Is a curse in a dead man's eye!
Seven days, seven nights, I saw that curse,
And yet I could not die.

'The moving Moon went up the sky,
And nowhere did abide:
Softly she was going up,
And a star or two beside –

'Her beams bemocked the sultry main,
Like April hoar-frost spread;
But where the ship's huge shadow lay,
The charmèd water burnt alway
A still and awful red.

By the light of the Moon he beholdeth God's creatures of the great calm.

'Beyond the shadow of the ship,
I watched the water-snakes:
They moved in tracks of shining white,
And when they reared, the elfish light
Fell off in hoary flakes.

'Within the shadow of the ship
I watched their rich attire:
Blue, glossy green, and velvet black,
They coiled and swam; and every track
Was a flash of golden fire.

Their beauty and their happiness.

'O happy living things! no tongue
Their beauty might declare:

He blesseth them in his heart.

A spring of love gushed from my heart,
And I blessed them unaware:
Sure my kind saint took pity on me,

And I blessed them unaware.

'The selfsame moment I could pray;
And from my neck so free
The Albatross fell off, and sank
Like lead into the sea.

The spell begins to break.

Part 5

'Oh sleep! it is a gentle thing,
Beloved from pole to pole!
To Mary Queen the praise be given!
She sent the gentle sleep from Heaven,
That slid into my soul.

'The silly buckets on the deck,
That had so long remained,
I dreamt that they were filled with dew;
And when I awoke, it rained.

By grace of the holy Mother, the ancient Mariner is refreshed with rain.

'My lips were wet, my throat was cold,
My garments all were dank;
Sure I had drunken in my dreams,
And still my body drank.

'I moved, and could not feel my limbs:
I was so light – almost
I thought that I had died in sleep,
And was a blessèd ghost.

'And soon I heard a roaring wind:
It did not come anear;
But with its sound it shook the sails,
That were so thin and sere.

He heareth sounds and seeth strange sights and commotions in the sky and the element.

'The upper air burst into life!
And a hundred fire-flags sheen,
To and fro they were hurried about!
And to and fro, and in and out,
The wan stars danced between.

'And the coming wind did roar more loud,
And the sails did sigh like sedge;
And the rain poured down from one black cloud;
The Moon was at its edge.

'The thick black cloud was cleft, and still
The Moon was at its side:
Like waters shot from some high crag,
The lightning fell with never a jag,
A river steep and wide.

The bodies of the ship's crew are inspirited, and the ship moves on;

'The loud wind never reached the ship.
Yet now the ship moved on!
Beneath the lightning and the Moon
The dead men gave a groan.

'They groaned, they stirred, they all uprose,
Nor spake, nor moved their eyes;
It had been strange, even in a dream,
To have seen those dead men rise.

'The helmsman steered, the ship moved on;
Yet never a breeze up blew;
The mariners all 'gan work the ropes,
Where they were wont to do;
They raised their limbs like lifeless tools –
We were a ghastly crew.

'The body of my brother's son
Stood by me, knee to knee:
The body and I pulled at one rope,
But he said nought to me.'

But not by the souls of the men, nor by demons of earth or middle air, but by a blessed troop of angelic spirits, sent

'I fear thee, ancient Mariner!'
'Be calm, thou Wedding-Guest!
'Twas not those souls that fled in pain,
Which to their corses came again,
But a troop of spirits blest:

'For when it dawned – they dropt their arms,

And clustered round the mast;
Sweet sounds rose slowly through their mouths,
And from their bodies passed.

down by the invocation of the guardian saint.

'Around, around, flew each sweet sound,
Then darted to the Sun;
Slowly the sounds came back again,
Now mixed, now one by one.

'Sometimes a-dropping from the sky
I heard the skylark sing;
Sometimes all little birds that are,
How they seemed to fill the sea and air
With their sweet jargoning!

'And now 'twas like all instruments,
Now like a lonely flute;
And now it is an angel's song,
That makes the Heavens be mute.

'It ceased; yet still the sails made on
A pleasant noise till noon,
A noise like of a hidden brook
In the leafy month of June,
That to the sleeping woods all night
Singeth a quiet tune.

'Till noon we quietly sailed on,
Yet never a breeze did breathe:
Slowly and smoothly went the ship,
Moved onward from beneath.

The lonesome Spirit from the South Pole carries on the ship as far as the Line, in obedience to the angelic troop, but still requireth vengeance.

'Under the keel nine fathom deep,
From the land of mist and snow,
The spirit slid: and it was he
That made the ship to go.
The sails at noon left off their tune,
And the ship stood still also.

'The Sun, right up above the mast,

Had fixed her to the ocean:
But in a minute she 'gan stir,
With a short uneasy motion –
Backwards and forwards half her length
With a short uneasy motion.

'Then, like a pawing horse let go,
She made a sudden bound:
It flung the blood into my head,
And I fell down in a swound.

The Polar Spirit's fellow-demons, the invisible inhabitants of the element, take part in his wrong; and two of them relate one to the other, that penance, long and heavy for the ancient Mariner hath been accorded to the Polar Spirit, who returneth southward.

'How long in that same fit I lay,
I have not to declare;
But ere my living life returned,
I heard and in my soul discerned
Two voices in the air.

' "Is it he?" quoth one, "Is this the man?
By him who died on cross,
With his cruel bow he laid full low
The harmless Albatross.

' "The Spirit who bideth by himself
In the land of mist and snow,
He loved the bird that loved the man
Who shot him with his bow."

'The other was a softer voice,
As soft as honeydew:
Quoth he, "The man hath penance done,
And penance more will do."

Part 6

First Voice
' "But tell me, tell me! speak again,
Thy soft response renewing –
What makes that ship drive on so fast!
What is the ocean doing?"

Second Voice
' "Still as a slave before his lord,
The Ocean hath no blast;
His great bright eye most silently
Up to the Moon is cast –

' "If he may know which way to go;
For she guides him smooth or grim.
See, brother, see! how graciously
She looketh down on him."

First Voice
' "But why drives on that ship so fast,
Without or wave or wind?"

The Mariner hath been cast into a trance; for the angelic power causeth the vessel to drive northward faster than human life could endure.

Second Voice
' "The air is cut away before,
And closes from behind.

' "Fly, brother, fly! more high, more high!
Or we shall be belated:
For slow and slow that ship will go,
When the Mariner's trance is abated."

The supernatural motion is retarded; the Mariner awakes, and his penance begins anew.

'I woke, and we were sailing on
As in a gentle weather:
'Twas night, calm night, the Moon was high;
The dead men stood together.

'All stood together on the deck,
For a charnel-dungeon fitter:
All fixed on me their stony eyes,
That in the Moon did glitter.

'The pang, the curse, with which they died,
Had never passed away:
I could not draw my eyes from theirs,
Nor turn them up to pray.

The curse is finally expiated.

'And now this spell was snapt: once more

I viewed the ocean green,
And looked far forth, yet little saw
Of what had else been seen –

Like one, that on a lonesome road
Doth walk in fear and dread,
And having once turned round walks on,
And turns no more his head;
Because he knows, a frightful fiend
Doth close behind him tread.

'But soon there breathed a wind on me,
Nor sound nor motion made:
Its path was not upon the sea,
In ripple or in shade.

'It raised my hair, it fanned my cheek
Like a meadow-gale of spring –
It mingled strangely with my fears,
Yet it felt like a welcoming.

'Swiftly, swiftly flew the ship,
Yet she sailed softly too:
Sweetly, sweetly blew the breeze –
On me alone it blew.

And the ancient Mariner beholdeth his native country.

'Oh! dream of joy! is this indeed
The lighthouse top I see?
Is this the hill? Is this the kirk?
Is this mine own countree?

'We drifted o'er the harbour bar,
And I with sobs did pray –
O let me be awake, my God!
Or let me sleep alway.

'The harbour-bay was clear as glass,
So smoothly it was strewn!
And on the bay the moonlight lay,
And the shadow of the Moon.

'The rock shone bright, the kirk no less,
That stands above the rock:
The moonlight steeped in silentness
The steady weathercock.

'And the bay was white with silent light,
Till rising from the same,
Full many shapes, that shadows were,
In crimson colours came.

The angelic spirits leave the dead bodies,

And appear in their own form soft light.

'A little distance from the prow
Those crimson shadows were:
I turned my eyes upon the deck –
Oh, Christ! what saw I there!

'Each corse lay flat, lifeless and flat,
And, by the holy rood!
A man all light, a seraph-man,
On every corse there stood.

'This seraph-band, each waved his hand:
It was a heavenly sight!
They stood as signals to the land,
Each one a lovely light;

'This seraph-band, each waved his hand,
No voice did they impart –
No voice; but oh! the silence sank
Like music on my heart.

'But soon I heard the dash of oars,
I heard the Pilot's cheer;
My head was turned perforce away,
And I saw a boat appear.

'The Pilot and the Pilot's boy,
I heard them coming fast:
Dear Lord in Heaven! it was a joy
The dead men could not blast.

'I saw a third – I heard his voice:
It is the Hermit good!
He singeth loud his godly hymns
That he makes in the wood.
He'll shrieve my soul, he'll wash away
The Albatross's blood.

Part 7

The Hermit of the Wood.

'This Hermit good lives in that wood
Which slopes down to the sea.
How loudly his sweet voice he rears!
He loves to talk with marineres
That come from a far countree.

'He kneels at morn, and noon, and eve –
He hath a cushion plump:
It is the moss that wholly hides
The rotted old oak-stump.

'The skiff-boat neared: I heard them talk,
"Why this is strange, I trow!
Where are those lights so many and fair,
That signal made but now?"

Approacheth the ship with wonder.

' "Strange, by my faith!" the Hermit said –
"And they answered not our cheer!
The planks look warped! and see those sails,
How thin they are and sere!
I never saw aught like to them,
Unless perchance it were

' "Brown skeletons of leaves that lag
My forest-brook along;
When the ivy-tod is heavy with snow,
And the owlet whoops to the wolf below,
That eats the she-wolf's young."

' "Dear Lord! it hath a fiendish look –"
(The Pilot made reply)

"I am a-feared" – "Push on, push on!"
Said the Hermit cheerily.

'The boat came closer to the ship,
But I nor spake nor stirred;
The boat came close beneath the ship,
And straight a sound was heard.

The ship suddenly sinketh.

'Under the water it rumbled on,
Still louder and more dread:
It reached the ship, it split the bay;
The ship went down like lead.

The ancient Mariner it saved in the Pilot's boat.

'Stunned by that loud and dreadful sound,
Which sky and ocean smote,
Like one that hath been seven days drowned
My body lay afloat;
But swift as dreams, myself I found
Within the Pilot's boat.

'Upon the whirl, where sank the ship,
The boat spun round and round;
And all was still, save that the hill
Was telling of the sound.

'I moved my lips – the Pilot shrieked
And fell down in a fit;
The holy Hermit raised his eyes,
And prayed where he did sit.

'I took the oars: the Pilot's boy,
Who now doth crazy go,
Laughed loud and long, and all the while
His eyes went to and fro.
"Ha! ha!" quoth he, "full plain I see,
The Devil knows how to row."

'And now, all in my own countree,
I stood on the firm land!
The Hermit stepped forth from the boat,

And scarcely he could stand.

The ancient mariner earnestly entreateth the Hermit to shrieve him; and the penance of life falls on him.

' "O shrieve me, shrieve me, holy man!"
The Hermit crossed his brow.
"Say quick," quoth he, "I bid thee say –
What manner of man art thou?"

'Forthwith this frame of mine was wrenched
With a woeful agony,
Which forced me to begin my tale;
And then it left me free.

And ever and anon throughout his future life an agony constraineth him to travel from land to land;

'Since then, at an uncertain hour,
That agony returns:
And till my ghastly tale is told,
This heart within me burns.

'I pass, like night, from land to land;
I have strange powers of speech;
That moment that his face I see,
I know the man that must hear me:
To him my tale I teach.

'What loud uproar bursts from that door!
The wedding-guests are there:
But in the garden-bower the bride
And bride-maids singing are:
And hark the little vesper bell,
Which biddeth me to prayer!

'O Wedding-Guest! this soul hath been
Alone on a wide wide sea:
So lonely 'twas, that God himself
Scarce seemed there to be.

'O sweeter than the marriage-feast,
'Tis sweeter far to me,
To walk together to the kirk
With a goodly company! –

'To walk together to the kirk,
And all together pray,
While each to his great Father bends,
Old men, and babes, and loving friends,
And youths and maidens gay!

'Farewell, farewell! but this I tell
To thee, thou Wedding-Guest!
He prayeth well, who loveth well
Both man and bird and beast.

And to teach, by his own example, love and reverence to all things that God made and loveth.

'He prayeth best, who loveth best
All things both great and small;
For the dear God who loveth us,
He made and loveth all.'

The Mariner, whose eye is bright,
Whose beard with age is hoar,
Is gone: and now the Wedding-Guest
Turned from the bridegroom's door.

He went like one that hath been stunned,
And is of sense forlorn:
A sadder and a wiser man,
He rose the morrow morn.

ROBERT SOUTHEY
Born 12 August 1774 : died 21 March 1843

The Old Woman of Berkeley

The Raven croak'd as she sate at her meal,
   And the Old Woman knew what he said,
And she grew pale at the Raven's tale,
   And sicken'd and went to her bed.

'Now fetch me my children, and fetch them with speed,'
  The Old Woman of Berkeley said,
'The Monk my son, and my daughter the Nun,
  Bid them hasten or I shall be dead.'

The Monk her son, and her daughter the Nun,
  Their way to Berkeley went,
And they have brought with pious thought
  The holy sacrament.

The Old Woman shriek'd as they enter'd her door,
  And she cried with a voice of despair,
'Now take away the sacrament,
  For its presence I cannot bear!'

Her lip it trembled with agony,
  The sweat ran down her brow,
'I have tortures in store for evermore,
  But spare me, my children, now!'

Away they sent the sacrament,
  The fit it left her weak,
She look'd at her children with ghastly eyes,
  And faintly struggled to speak.

'All kind of sin I have rioted in,
  And the judgement now must be,
But I secured my children's souls,
  Oh! pray, my children, for me!

'I have 'nointed myself with infant's fat,
  The fiends have been my slaves,
From sleeping babes I have suck'd the breath,
  And breaking by charms the sleep of death,
I have call'd the dead from their graves.

'And the Devil will fetch me now in fire,
  My witchcrafts to atone;
And I who have troubled the dead man's grave
  Shall never have rest in my own.

'Bless, I entreat, my winding sheet,
  My children, I beg of you;
And with holy water sprinkle my shroud,
  And sprinkle my coffin too.

'And let me be chain'd in my coffin of stone,
  And fasten it strong, I implore,
With iron bars, and with three chains,
  Chain it to the church floor.

'And bless the chains and sprinkle them,
  And let fifty Priests stand round,
Who night and day the mass may say
  Where I lie on the ground.

'And see that fifty Choristers
  Beside the bier attend me,
And day and night by the tapers' light,
  With holy hymns defend me.

'Let the church bells all, both great and small
  Be toll'd by night and day,
To drive from thence the fiends who come
  To bear my body away.

'And ever have the church door barr'd
  After the even-song;
And I beseech you, children dear,
  Let the bars and bolts be strong.

'And let this be three days and nights
  My wretched corpse to save;
Till the fourth morning keep me safe,
  And then I may rest in my grave.'

The Old Woman of Berkeley laid her down,
  And her eyes grew deadly dim,
Short came her breath, and the struggle of death
  Did loosen every limb.

They blest the old woman's winding sheet,
  With rites and prayers due,
With holy water they sprinkled her shroud,
  And they sprinkled her coffin too.

And they chain'd her in her coffin of stone,
  And with iron barr'd it down,
And in the church with three strong chains
  They chain'd it to the ground.

And they blest the chains and sprinkled them,
  And fifty Priests stood round,
By night and day the Mass to say
  Where she lay on the ground.

And fifty sacred Choristers
  Beside the bier attend her,
Who day and night by the tapers' light
  Should with holy hymns defend her.

To see the Priests and Choristers
  It was a goodly sight,
Each holding, as it were a staff,
  A taper burning bright.

And the church bells all, both great and small,
  Did toll so loud and long;
And they have barr'd the church door hard,
  After the even-song.

And the first night the tapers' light
  Burnt steadily and clear,
But they without a hideous rout
  Of angry fiends could hear;

A hideous roar at the church door
  Like a long thunder peal;
And the Priests they pray'd, and the Choristers sung
  Louder in fearful zeal.

Loud toll'd the bell, the Priests pray'd well,
  The tapers they burnt bright,
The Monk her son, and her daughter the Nun,
  They told their beads all night.

The cock he crew, the Fiends they flew
  From the voice of the morning away;
Then undisturb'd the Choristers sing,
  And the fifty Priests they pray;
As they had sung and pray'd all night,
  They pray'd and sung all day.

The second night the tapers' light
  Burnt dismally and blue,
And every one saw his neighbour's face
  Like a dead man's face to view.

And yells and cries without arise
  That the stoutest heart might shock,
And a deafening roaring like a cataract pouring
  Over a mountain rock.

The Monk and the Nun they told their beads
  As fast as they could tell,
And aye as louder grew the noise
  The faster went the bell.

Louder and louder the Choristers sung
  As they trembled more and more,
And the Priests as they pray'd to heaven for aid,
  They smote their breasts full sore.

The cock he crew, the Fiends they flew
  From the voice of the morning away;
The undisturb'd the Choristers sing,
  And the fifty Priests they pray;
As they had sung and pray'd all night,
  They pray'd and sung all day.

The third night came, and the tapers' flame

A frightful stench did make;
And they burnt as though they had been dipt
In the burning brimstone lake.

And the loud commotion, like the rushing of ocean,
Grew momently more and more;
And strokes as of a battering ram
Did shake the strong church door.

The bellmen, they for very fear
Could toll the bell no longer;
And still as louder grew the strokes
Their fear it grew the stronger.

The Monk and the Nun forgot their beads,
They fell on the ground in dismay;
There was not a single Saint in heaven
To whom they did not pray.

And the Choristers' song, which late was so strong,
Falter'd with consternation,
For the church did rock as an earthquake shock
Uplifted its foundation.

And a sound was heard like the trumpet's blast,
That shall one day wake the dead;
The strong church door could bear no more,
And the bolts and the bars they fled.

And the tapers' light was extinguish'd quite,
And the Choristers faintly sung,
And the Priests dismay'd, panted and pray'd,
And on all Saints in heaven for aid
They call'd with trembling tongue.

And in He came with eyes of flame,
The Devil to fetch the dead,
And all the church with his presence glow'd
Like a fiery furnace red.

He laid his hand on the iron chains,
  And like flax they moulder'd asunder,
And the coffin lid, which was barr'd so firm,
  He burst with his voice of thunder.

And He bade the Old Woman of Berkeley rise,
  And come with her Master away;
A cold sweat started on that cold corpse,
  At the voice she was forced to obey.

She rose on her feet in her winding sheet,
  Her dead flesh quiver'd with fear,
And a groan like that which the Old Woman gave
  Never did mortal hear.

She follow'd her Master to the church door,
  There stood a black horse there;
His breath was red like furnace smoke,
  His eyes like a meteor's glare.

The Devil he flung her on the horse,
  And he leapt up before,
And away like the lightning's speed they went,
  And she was seen no more.

They saw her no more, but her cries
  For four miles round they could hear,
And children at rest at their mother's breast
  Started, and scream'd with fear.

MATTHEW GREGORY LEWIS

born 9 July 1775 : died 14 May 1818

Alonzo the Brave and Fair Imogene

A warrior so bold and a virgin so bright
  Conversed, as they sat on the green;
They gazed on each other with tender delight:
Alonzo the Brave was the name of the Knight,
  The maid's was the Fair Imogene.

'And, oh!' said the youth, 'since to-morrow I go
  To fight in a far distant land,
Your tears for my absence soon leaving to flow,
Some others will court you, and you will bestow
  On a wealthier suitor your hand.'

'Oh! hush these suspicions,' Fair Imogene said,
  'Offensive to love and to me!
For, if you be living, or if you be dead,
I swear by the Virgin, that none in your stead
  Shall husband of Imogene be.

'And if e'er for another my heart should decide,
  Forgetting Alonzo the Brave,
God grant, that, to punish my falsehood and pride,
Your ghost at the marriage may sit by my side,
May tax me with perjury, claim me as bride,
  And bear me away to the grave!'

To Palestine hastened the hero so bold;
  His love she lamented him sore:
But scarce had a twelvemonth elapsed, when behold,
A Baron all covered with jewels and gold
  Arrived at Fair Imogene's door.

His treasure, his presents, his spacious domain,
  Soon made her untrue to her vows;

He dazzled her eyes; he bewildered her brain;
He caught her affections so light and so vain,
  And carried her home as his spouse.

And now had the marriage been blessed by the priest;
  The revelry now was begun:
The tables they groaned with the weight of the feast;
Nor yet had the laughter and merriment ceased,
  When the bell of the castle tolled – 'one!'

Then first with amazement Fair Imogene found
  That a stranger was placed by her side:
His air was terrific; he uttered no sound;
He spoke not, he moved not, he looked not around,
  But earnestly gazed on the bride.

His vizor was closed, and gigantic his height;
  His armour was sable to view;
All pleasure and laughter were hushed at his sight;
The dogs, as they eyed him, drew back in affright;
  The light in the chamber burnt blue!

His presence all bosoms appeared to dismay;
  The guests sat in silence and fear:
At length spoke the bride, while she trembled – 'I pray,
Sir Knight, that your helmet aside you would lay,
  And deign to partake of our cheer.'

The lady is silent: the stranger complies,
  His vizor he slowly unclosed;
Oh! then what a sight met Fair Imogene's eyes!
What words can express her dismay and surprise,
  When a skeleton's head was exposed!

All present then uttered a terrified shout;
  All turned with disgust from the scene.
The worms they crept in, and the worms they crept out,
And sported his eyes and his temples about,
  While the spectre addressed Imogene:

'Behold me, thou false one! behold me!' he cried;
'Remember Alonzo the Brave!
God grants, that, to punish they falsehood and pride,
My ghost at thy marriage should sit by thy side,
Should tax thee with perjury, claim thee as bride,
And bear thee away to the grave!'

Thus saying, his arms round the lady he wound,
While loudly she shrieked in dismay;
Then sank with his prey through the wide-yawning ground:
Nor ever again was Fair Imogene found,
Or the spectre who bore her away.

Not long lived the Baron: and none since that time
To inhabit the castle presume;
For chronicles tell, that, by order sublime,
There Imogene suffers the pain of her crime,
And mourns her deplorable doom.

At midnight four times in each year does her sprite,
When mortals in slumber are bound,
Arrayed in her bridal apparel of white,
Appear in the hall with the skeleton-knight,
And shriek as he whirls her around.

While they drink out of skulls newly torn from the grave,
Dancing round them pale spectres are seen:
Their liquor is blood, and this horrible stave
They howl: 'To the health of Alonza the Brave,
And his consort the False Imogene!'

from *The Monk*

HENRY KIRKE WHITE
born 21 March 1785 : died 19 October 1806

The Dance of the Consumptives

Ding-dong! ding-dong;
Merry, merry, go the bells,
Ding-dong! ding-dong!
Over the heath, over the moor, and over the dale
Swinging slow with sullen roar,
Dance, dance away, the jocund roundelay!
Ding-dong, ding-dong, calls us away.

2.
Round the oak, and round the elm,
Merrily foot it o'er the ground!
The sentry ghost it stands aloof,
So merrily, merrily, foot it round.
Ding-dong! ding-dong
Merry, merry, got the bells,
Swelling in the nightly gale,
The sentry ghost,
It keeps its post,
And soon, and soon our sports must fail:
But let us trip the nightly ground,
While the merry, merry, bells rings round.

3.
Hark! hark! the death-watch ticks!
See, see, the winding-sheet!
Our dance is done,
Our race is run,
And we must lie at the alder's feet
Ding-dong, ding-dong,
Merry, merry, go the bells,
Swinging o'er the weltering wave!

And we must seek
Our deathbeds bleak,
Where the green sod grows upon the grave.

from *Fragment of an Eccentric Drama*

GEORGE GORDON, LORD BYRON
born 22 January 1788 : died 19 April 1824

The Incantation

When the moon is on the wave,
And the glow-worm in the grass,
And the meteor on the grave,
And the wisp on the morass;
When the falling stars are shooting,
And the answered owls are hooting,
And the silent leaves are still
In the shadow of the hill,
Shall my soul be upon thine,
With a power and with a sign.

Though thy slumber may be deep,
Yet thy spirit shall not sleep,
There are shades which will not vanish,
There are thoughts thou canst not banish;
By a power to thee unknown,
Thou canst never be alone;
Thou art wrapt as with a shroud,
Thou art gathered in a cloud;
And for ever shalt thou dwell
In the spirit of this spell.

Though thou seest me not pass by,
Thou shalt feel me with thine eye

As a thing that, though unseen,
Must be near thee, and hath been;
And when in that secret dread
Thou hast turn'd around thy head,
Thou shalt marvel I am not
As thy shadow on the spot,
And the power which thou dost feel
Shall be what thou must conceal.

And a magic voice and verse
Hath baptized thee with a curse;
And a spirit of the air
Hath begirt thee with a snare;
In the wind there is a voice
Shall forbid thee to rejoice;
And to thee shall Night deny
All the quiet of her sky;
And the day shall have a sun,
Which shall make thee wish it done.

From thy false tears I did distil
An essence which hath strength to kill;
From thy own heart I then did wring
The black blood in its blackest spring;
From thy own smile I snatched the snake,
For there it coil'd as in a brake;
From thy own lip I drew the charm
Which gave all these their chiefest harm;
In proving every poison known,
I found the strongest was thine own.

By thy cold breast and serpent smile,
By thy unfathom'd gulfs of guile,
By that most seeming virtuous eye,
By thy shut soul's hypocrisy;
By the perfection of thine art
Which pass'd for human thine own heart;
By thy delight in others' pain,
And by thy brotherhood of Cain,
I call upon thee! and compel

Thyself to be thy proper Hell!

And on thy head I pour the vial
Which doth devote thee to this trial;
Nor to slumber, nor to die,
Shall be in thy destiny;
Though thy death shall still seem near
To thy wish, but as a fear;
Lo! the spell now works around thee,
And the clankless chain hath bound thee;
O'er thy heart and brain together
Hath the word been pass'd – now wither!

from *Manfred, Act 1, Scene 1*

PERCY BYSSHE SHELLEY
born 4 August 1792 : died 8 July 1822

Arethusa

Arethusa arose
From her couch of snows
In the Acroceraunian mountains, –
From cloud and from crag,
With many a jag,
Shepherding her bright fountains.
She leapt down the rocks
With her rainbow locks
Streaming among the streams; –
Her steps paved with green
The downward ravine
Which slopes to the western gleams:
And gliding and springing,
She went, ever singing,
In murmurs as soft as sleep;

The Earth seemed to love her,
And Heaven smiled above her,
As she lingered towards the deep.

Then Alpheus bold,
On his glacier cold,
With his trident the mountains strook;
And opened a chasm
In the rocks; – with the spasm
All Erymanthus shook.
And the black south wind
It concealed behind
The urns of the silent snow,
And earthquake and thunder
Did rend in sunder
The bars of the springs below:
The beard and the hair
Of the river God were
Seen through the torrent's sweep,
As he followed the light
Of the fleet nymph's flight
To the brink of the Dorian deep.

'Oh, save me! Oh, guide me!
And bid the deep hide me,
For he grasps me now by the hair!'
The loud Ocean heard,
To its blue depth stirred,
And divided at her prayer;
And under the water
The Earth's white daughter
Fled like a sunny beam,
Behind her descended,
Her billows unblended
With the brackish Dorian stream: –
Like a gloomy stain
On the emerald main
Alpheus rushed behind, –
As an eagle pursuing
A dove to its ruin

Down the streams of the cloudy wind.

Under the bowers
Where the Ocean Powers
Sit on their pearled thrones,
Through the coral woods
Of the weltering floods,
Over heaps of unvalued stones:
Through the dim beams
Which amid the streams
Weave a net-work of coloured light;
And under the caves,
Where the shadowy waves
Are as green as the forest's night:–
Outspeeding the shark,
And the sword-fish dark,
Under the ocean foam,
And up through the rifts
Of the mountain clifts
They passed to their Dorian home.

And now from their fountains
In Enna's mountains,
Down one vale where the morning basks,
Like friends once parted
Grown single-hearted,
They ply their watery tasks.
At sun-rise they leap
From their cradles steep
In the cave of the shelving hill;
At noon-tide they flow
Through the woods below
And the meadows of Asphodel;
And at night they sleep
In the rocking deep
Beneath the Ortygian shore; –
Like spirits that lie
In the azure sky
When they love but live no more.

JOHN KEATS
born 31 October 1795 : died 23 February 1821

La Belle Dame Sans Merci

O what can ail thee, knight-at-arms,
  Alone and palely loitering?
The sedge has wither'd from the lake,
  And no birds sing.

O what can ail thee, knight-at-arms!
  So haggard and so woe-begone?
The squirrel's granary is full,
  And the harvest's done.

I see a lily on thy brow
  With anguish moist and fever dew,
And on thy cheeks a fading rose
  Fast withereth too.

I met a lady in the meads,
  Full beautiful – a faery's child,
Her hair was long, her foot was light,
  And her eyes were wild.

I made a garland for her head,
  And bracelets too, and fragrant zone;
She look'd at me as she did love,
  And made sweet moan.

I set her on my pacing steed,
  And nothing else saw all day long,
For sidelong would she bend, and sing
  A faery's song.

She found me roots of relish sweet,
  And honey wild, and manna dew,

And sure in language strange she said –
'I love thee true.'

She took me to her elfin grot,
And there she wept, and sigh'd full sore,
And there I shut her wild wild eyes
With kisses four.

And there she lulled me asleep,
And there I dream'd – Ah! woe betide!
The latest dream I ever dream'd
On the cold hill's side.

I saw pale kings and princes too,
Pale warriors, death-pale were they all;
They cried – 'La Belle Dame sans Merci
Hath thee in thrall!'

I saw their starved lips in the gloam,
With horrid warning gaped wide,
And I awoke and found me here,
On the cold hill's side.

And this is why I sojourn here,
Alone and palely loitering,
Though the sedge is wither'd from the lake,
And no birds sing.

THOMAS HOOD
born 23 May 1799 : died 3 May 1845

The Haunted House

'A jolly place, said he, in days of old,
But something ails it now: the spot is curst.'

Wordsworth

Part 1

Some dreams we have are nothing else but dreams,
Unnatural, and full of contradictions;
Yet others of our most romantic schemes
Are something more than fictions.

It might be only on enchanted ground;
It might be merely by a thought's expansion;
But in the spirit, or the flesh, I found
An old deserted Mansion.

A residence for woman, child, and man,
A dwelling place, – and yet no habitation;
A House, – but under some prodigious ban
Of excommunication.

Unhinged the iron gates half open hung,
Jarr'd by the gusty gales of many winters,
That from its crumbled pedestal had flung
One marble globe in splinters.

No dog was at the threshold, great or small;
No pigeon on the roof – no household creature –
No cat demurely dozing on the wall –
Not one domestic feature.

No human figure stirr'd, to go or come,
No face look'd forth from shut or open casement;
No chimney smoked – there was no sign of Home
From parapet to basement.

With shatter'd panes the grassy court was starr'd;
The time-worn coping-stone had tumbled after;
And thro' the ragged roof the sky shone, barr'd
With naked beam and rafter.

O'er all there hung a shadow and a fear;
A sense of mystery the spirit daunted,
And said, as plain as whisper in the ear,
The place is Haunted!

The flow'r grew wild and rankly as the weed,
Roses with thistles struggled for espial,
And vagrant plants of parasitic breed
Had overgrown the Dial.

But gay or gloomy, steadfast or infirm,
No heart was there to heed the hour's duration;
All times and tides were lost in one long term
Of stagnant desolation.

The wren had built within the Porch, she found
Its quiet loneliness so sure and thorough;
And on the lawn, – within its turfy mound, –
The rabbit made his burrow.

The rabbit wild and gray, that flitted thro'
The shrubby clumps, and frisk'd, and sat, and vanish'd,
But leisurely and bold, as if he knew
His enemy was banish'd.

The wary crow, – the pheasant from the woods –
Lull'd by the still and everlasting sameness,
Close to the Mansion, like domestic broods,
Fed with a "shocking tameness."

The coot was swimming in the reedy pond,
Beside the water-hen, so soon affrighted;
And in the weedy moat the heron, fond
of solitude, alighted.

The moping heron, motionless and stiff,
That on a stone, as silently and stilly,
Stood, an apparent sentinel, as if
To guard the water-lily.

No sound was heard except, from far away,
The ringing of the Whitwall's shrilly laughter,
Or, now and then, the chatter of the jay,
That Echo murmur'd after.

But Echo never mock'd the human tongue;
Some weighty crime, that Heaven could not pardon,
A secret curse on that old Building hung,
And its deserted Garden.

The beds were all untouch'd by hand or tool;
No footstep marked the damp and mossy gravel,
Each walk as green as is the mantled pool,
For want of human travel.

The vine unprun'd, and the neglected peach,
Droop'd from the wall with which they used to grapple;
And on the canker'd tree, in easy reach,
Rotted the golden apple.

But awfully the truant shunn'd the ground,
The vagrant keep aloof, and daring Poacher;
In spite of gaps that thro' the fences round
Invited the encroacher.

For over all there hung a cloud of fear,
A sense of mystery the spirit daunted,
And said, as plain as whisper in the ear,
The place is Haunted!

The pear and quince lay squander'd on the grass;
The mould was purple with unheeded showers
Of bloomy plums – a Wilderness it was
Of fruits, and weeds, and flowers!

The marigold amidst the nettles blew,
The gourd embraced the rose bush in its ramble,
The thistle and the stock together grew,
The holly-hock and bramble.

The bear-bine with the lilac interlac'd,
The sturdy burdock choked its slender neighbour,
The spicy pink. All tokens were effac'd
Of human care and labour.

The very yew Formality had train'd
To such a rigid pyramidal stature,
For want of trimming had almost regain'd
The raggedness of nature.

The Fountain was a-dry – neglect and time
Had marr'd the work of artisan and mason,
And efts and croaking frogs, begot of slime,
Sprawl'd in the ruin'd bason.

The Statue, fallen from its marble base,
Amidst the refuse leaves, and herbage rotten,
Lay like the Idol of some by-gone race,
Its name and rites forgotten.

On ev'ry side the aspect was the same,
All ruin'd, desolate, forlorn, and savage:
No hand or foot within the precinct came
To rectify or ravage.

For over all there hung a cloud of fear,
A sense of mystery the spirit daunted,
And said as plain as whisper in the ear,
The place is Haunted!

Part 2

O, very gloomy is the House of Woe,
Where tears are falling while the bell is knelling,
With all the dark solemnities which show
That Death is in the dwelling!

O very, very dreary is the room
Where Love, domestic Love, no longer nestles,
But smitten by the common stroke of doom,
The Corpse lies on the trestles!

But House of Woe, and hearse, and sable pall,
The narrow home of the departed mortal,
Ne'er look'd so gloomy as that Ghostly Hall,
With its deserted portal!

The centipede along the threshold crept,
The cobweb hung across in mazy tangle,
And in its winding-sheet the maggot slept,
At every nook and angle.

The keyhole lodg'd the earwig and her brood,
The emmets of the steps had old possession,
And march'd in search of their diurnal food
In undisturb'd procession.

As undisturbed as the prehensile cell
Of moth or maggot, or the spider's tissue,
For never foot upon that threshold fell,
To enter or to issue.

O'er all there hung the shadow of a fear,
A sense of mystery the spirit daunted,
And said, as plain as whisper in the ear,
The place is Haunted.

Howbeit, the door I pushed – or so I dream'd –
Which slowly, slowly gaped, – the hinges creaking
With such a rusty eloquence, it seem'd
That Time himself was speaking.

But Time was dumb within that Mansion old,
Or left his tale to the heraldic banners
That hung from the corroded walls, and told
Of former men and manners.

Those tatter'd flags, that with the open'd door,
Seem'd the old wave of battle to remember,
While fallen fragments danc'd upon the floor
Like dead leaves in December.

The startled bats flew out – bird after bird –
The screech-owl overhead began to flutter,
And seem'd to mock the cry that she had heard
Some dying victim utter!

A shriek that echoed from the joisted roof,
And up the stair, and further still and further,
Till in some ringing chamber far aloof
It ceased its tale of murther!

Meanwhile the rusty armour rattled round,
The banner shudder'd, and the ragged streamer;
All things the horrid tenor of the sound
Acknowledged with a tremor.

The antlers, where the helmet hung and belt,
Stirr'd as the tempest stirs the forest branches,
Or as the stag had trembled when he felt
The blood-hound at his haunches.

The window jingled in its crumbled frame,
And thro' its many gaps of destitution
Dolorous moans and hollow sighings came,
Like those of dissolution.

The wood-louse dropped, and rolled into a ball,
Touch'd by some impulse occult or mechanic;
And nameless beetles ran along the wall
In universal panic.

The subtle spider, that from overhead
Hung like a spy on human guilt and error,
Suddenly turn'd, and up its slender thread
Ran with a nimble terror.

The very stains and fractures on the wall
Assuming features solemn and terrific,
Hinted some Tragedy of that old Hall,
Lock'd up in hieroglyphic.

Some tale that might, perchance, have solv'd the doubt,
Wherefore amongst those flags so dull and livid,
The Banner of the BLOODY HAND shone out
So ominously vivid.

Some key to that inscrutable appeal,
Which made the very frame of Nature quiver;
And ev'ry thrilling nerve and fibre feel
So ague-like a shiver.

For over all there hung a cloud of fear,
A sense of mystery the spirit daunted;
And said, as plain as whisper in the ear,
The place is Haunted!

If but a rat had lingered in the house,
To lure the thought into a social channel!
But not a rat remain'd, or tiny mouse,
To squeak behind the pannel.

Huge drops roll'd down the walls, as if they wept;
And where the cricket used to chirp so shrilly,
The toad was squatting, and the lizard crept
On that damp hearth and chilly.

For years no cheerful blaze had sparkled there,
Or glanc'd on coat of buff or knightly metal;
The slug was crawling on the vacant chair, –
The snail upon the settle.

The floor was redolent of mould and must,
The fungus in the rotten seams had quickened;
While on the oaken table coats of dust
Perennially had thicken'd.

No mark of leathern jack or metal can,
No cup – no horn – no hospitable token, –
All social ties between that board and Man
Had long ago been broken.

There was so foul a rumour in the air,
The shadow of a Presence so atrocious;
No human creature could have feasted there,
Even the most ferocious.

For over all there hung a cloud of fear,
A sense of mystery the spirit daunted,
And said, as plain as whisper in the ear,
The place is Haunted!

Part 3

'Tis hard for human actions to account,
Whether from reason or from impulse only –
But some internal prompting bade me mount
The gloomy stairs and lonely.

Those gloomy stairs, so dark, and damp, and cold,
With odours as from bones and relics carnal,
Deprived of rite, and consecrated mould,
The chapel vault, or charnel.

Those dreary stairs, where with the sounding stress
Of ev'ry step so many echoes blended,
The mind, with dark misgivings, fear'd to guess
How many feet ascended.

The tempest with its spoils had drifted in,
Till each unwholesome stone was darkly spotted,
As thickly as the leopard's dappled skin,
With leaves that rankly rotted.

The air was thick – and in the upper gloom
The bat – or something in its shape – was winging;
And on the wall, as chilly as a tomb,
The Death's-Head moth was clinging

That mystic moth, which, with a sense profound
Of all unholy presence, augurs truly;
And with a grim significance flits round
The taper burning bluely.

Such omens in the place there seem'd to be,
At ev'ry crooked turn, or on the landing,
The straining eyeball was prepar'd to see
Some Apparition standing.

For over all there hung a cloud of fear,
A sense of mystery the spirit daunted,
And said, as plain as whisper in the ear,
The place is Haunted!

Yet no portentous Shape the sight amaz'd;
Each object plain, and tangible, and valid;
But from their tarnish'd frames dark Figures gaz'd,
And Faces spectre-pallid.

Not merely with the mimic life that lies
Within the compass of Art's simulation;
Their souls were looking thro' their painted eyes
With awful speculation.

On ev'ry lip a speechless horror dwelt;
On ev'ry brow the burthen of affliction;
The old Ancestral Spirits knew and felt
The House's malediction.

Such earnest woe their features overcast,
They might have stirr'd, or sigh'd, or wept, or spoken;
But, save the hollow moaning of the blast,
The stillness was unbroken.

No other sound or stir of life was there,
Except my steps in solitary clamber,
From flight to flight, from humid stair to stair,
From chamber into chamber.

Deserted rooms of luxury and state,
That old magnificence had richly furnish'd
With pictures, cabinets of ancient date,
And carvings gilt and burnish'd.

Rich hangings, storied by the needle's art,
With scripture history, or classic fable;
But all had faded, save one ragged part,
Where Cain was slaying Abel.

The silent waste of mildew and the moth
Had marr'd the tissue with a partial ravage;
But undecaying frown'd upon the cloth
Each feature stern and savage.

The sky was pale; the cloud a thing of doubt;
Some hues were fresh, and some decay'd and duller;
But still the BLOODY HAND shone strangely out
With vehemence of colour!

The BLOODY HAND that with a lurid stain
Shone on the dusty floor, a dismal token,
Projected from the casement's painted pane,
Where all beside was broken.

The BLOODY HAND significant of crime,
That glaring on the old heraldic banner,
Had kept its crimson unimpair'd by time,
In such a wondrous manner!

O'er all there hung the shadow of a fear,
A sense of mystery the spirit daunted,
And said, as plain as whisper in the ear,
The place is Haunted!

The Death Watch ticked behind the pannel'd oak,
Inexplicable tremors shook the arras,
And echoes strange and mystical awoke,
The fancy to embarrass.

Prophetic hints that filled the soul with dread,
But thro' one gloomy entrance pointing mostly,
The while some secret inspiration said,
That Chamber is the Ghostly!

Across the door no gossamer festoon
Swung pendulous – no web – no dusty fringes,
No silky chrysalis or white cocoon
About its nooks and hinges.

The spider shunn'd the interdicted room,
The moth, the beetle, and the fly were banish'd,
And where the sunbeam fell athwart the gloom
The very midge had vanish'd.

One lonely ray that glanc'd upon a Bed,
As if with awful aim direct and certain,
To show the BLOODY HAND in burning red
Embroider'd on the curtain.

And yet no gory stain was on the quilt –
The pillow in its place had slowly rotted;
The floor alone retain'd the trace of guilt,
Those boards obscurely spotted.

Obscurely spotted to the door, and thence
With mazy doubles to the grated casement –
Oh what a tale they told of fear intense,
Of horror and amazement!

What human creature in the dead of night
Had cours'd like hunted hare that cruel distance?
Had sought the door, the window in his flight,
Striving for dear existence?

What shrieking Spirit in that bloody room
Its mortal frame had violently quitted? –
Across the sunbeam, with a sudden gloom,
A ghostly Shadow flitted.

Across the sunbeam, and along the wall,
But painted on the air so very dimly,
It hardly veil'd the tapestry at all,
Or portrait frowning grimly.

O'er all there hung the shadow of a fear,
A sense of mystery the spirit daunted,
And said, as plain as whisper in the ear,
The place is Haunted!

RICHARD HENRY HORNE
born 1 January 1803 : died 13 March 1884

The Doomed Giants

Now Phoibos through the cave
Sent a broad ray! Harpax arose, and then, –
Pondering on rules for safest monarchy, –
Encolyon heavily. The solar beam
Filled the great cave with radiance equable,
And not a cranny held one speck of shade.
A moony halo round Orion came,
As of some pure protecting influence,
While with intense light glared the walls and roof,
The heat increasing. The three giants stood
With glazing eyes, fixed. Terribly the light
Beat on the dazzled stone, and the cave hummed
With reddening heat, till the red hair and beard
Of Harpax shewed no difference from the rest,
Which once were iron-black. The sullen walls
Then smouldered down to steady oven-heat,
Like that with care attained when bread has ceased
Its steaming, and displays an angry tan.
The appalled faces of the giants shewed
Full consciousness of their immediate doom.

And soon the cave a potter's furnace glowed,
Or kiln for largest bricks, and thus remained
The while Orion, in his halo clasped
By some invisible power, beheld the clay,
Of these his early friends, change. Life was gone!

Now sank the heat – the cave-walls lost their glare –
The red lights faded, and the halo pale
Around him, into chilly air expanded.
There stood the three giant images, in hue
Of chalky white and red, like those strange shapes
In Egypt's ancient tombs; but presently
Each visage and each form with cracks and flaws
Was seamed, and the lost countenance brake up,
As, with brief toppling, forward prone they fell, –
And in dismay uttering a sudden cry,
Orion headlong from the cavern fled.

The Slaying of the Monsters

O'er the far rocks, midst gorge and glen profound;
Now from close thickets, now from grassy plains;
The sounds of raging contest, flight and death
Told where Rhexergon and Biastor wrought
Their well-directed work. Them, quickly joined
Their head in this destruction, and ere night,
Huge forms, ferocious, mighty in the dawn,
When hoar rime glistened on each hairy shape,
Nought fearing, swift, brimfull of raging life,
Lay stiffening in black pools of jellied gore.
Nor with the day ceased their tremendous task,
But all night long Orion led the way
Through moonless passes to most secret lairs,
Where in their deep abodes fierce monsters crouched, –
Dragons, and sea-beasts, and compounded forms, –
And in the pitchy blackness madly huddling,
Midst deafening yells and hisses they were slain.

from *ORION: Book 2, Canto 2*

THOMAS LOVELL BEDDOES
born 20 July 1803 : died 26 January 1849

The Phantom-Wooer

1
A ghost, that loved a lady fair,
Ever in the starry air
   Of midnight at her pillow stood;
And, with a sweetness skies above
The luring words of human love,
   Her soul the phantom wooed.
Sweet and sweet is their poisoned note,
The little snakes of silver throat,
In mossy skulls that nest and lie,
Ever singing 'die, oh! die.'

2
Young soul, put off your flesh, and come
With me into the quiet tomb,
   Our bed is lovely, dark and sweet;
The earth will swing us, as she goes,
Beneath our coverlid of snows,
   And the warm leaden sheet.
Dear and dear is their poisoned note,
The little snakes of silver throat,
In mossy skulls that nest and lie,
Ever singing 'die, oh! die.'

The Old Ghost

Over the water an old ghost strode
   To a churchyard on the shore,
And over him the waters had flowed
   A thousand years or more,
And pale and wan and weary

Looked never a sprite as he;
For it's lonely and it's dreary
The ghost of a body to be
That has mouldered away in the sea.

Over the billows the old ghost stepped,
And the winds in mockery sung;
For the bodiless ghost would fain have wept
Over the maiden that lay so young
'Mong the thistles and toadstools so hoary.
And he begged of the waves a tear,
But they shook upwards their moonlight glory,
And the shark looked on with a sneer
At his yearning desire and agony.

HENRY WADSWORTH LONGFELLOW
born 27 February 1807 : died 24 March 1882

The Ghosts of the Departed

From his couch rose Hiawatha,
From his shaggy hides of bison,
Pushed aside the deer-skin curtain,
Saw the pallid guests, the shadows,
Sitting upright on their couches,
Weeping in the silent midnight.
And he said: 'O guests! why is it
That your hearts are so afflicted,
That you sob so in the midnight?
Has perchance the old Nokomis,
Has my wife, my Minnehaha,
Wronged or grieved you by unkindness,
Failed in hospitable duties?'
Then the shadows ceased from weeping,
Ceased from sobbing and lamenting,

And they said with gentle voices,
'We are ghosts of the departed,
Souls of those who once were with you.
From the realms of Chibiabos
Hither have we come to try you,
Hither have we come to warn you.
'Cries of grief and lamentation
Reach us in the Blessed Islands;
Cries of anguish from the living,
Calling back their friends departed,
Sadden us with useless sorrow.
Therefore have we come to try you;
No one knows us, no one heeds us.
We are but a burden to you,
And we see that the departed
Have no place among the living.
'Think of this, O Hiawatha!
Speak of it to all the people,
That henceforward and forever
They no more with lamentations
Sadden the souls of the departed
In the Islands of the Blessed.
'Do not lay such heavy burdens,
In the graves of those you bury,
Not such weight of furs and wampum,
Not such weight of pots and kettles,
For the spirits faint beneath them.
Only give them food to carry,
Only give them fire to light them.
'Four days in the spirit's journey
To the land of ghosts and shadows,
Four its lonely night encampments;
Four times must their fires by lighted.
Therefore, when the dead are buried,
Let a fire, as night approaches,
Four times on the grave be kindled,
That the soul upon its journey
May not lack the cheerful firelight,
May not grope about in darkness.
'Farewell, noble Hiawatha!

We have put you to the trial,
To the proof have put your patience,
By the insult of our presence,
By the outrage of our actions.
We have found you great and noble.
Fail not in the greater trial,
Faint not in the harder struggle.'
  When they ceased, a sudden darkness
Fell and filled the silent wigwam.
Hiawatha heard a rustle
As of garments trailing by him,
Heard the curtain of the doorway
Lifted by a hand he saw not,
Felt the cold breath of the night air,
For a moment saw the starlight;
But he saw the ghosts no longer,
Saw no more the wandering spirits
From the kingdom of Ponemah,
From the land of the Hereafter.

from *The Song of Hiawatha*

EDGAR ALLAN POE
born 19 January 1809 : died 7 October 1849

The City in the Sea

Lo! Death has reared himself a throne
In a strange city lying alone
Far down within the dim West,
Where the good and the bad and the worst and the best
Have gone to their eternal rest.
There shrines and palaces and towers
(Time-eaten towers that tremble not!)
Resemble nothing that is ours.

Around, by lifting winds forgot,
Resignedly beneath the sky
The melancholy waters lie.

No rays from the holy heaven come down
On the long night-time of that town;
But light from out the lurid sea
Streams up the turrets silently –
Gleams up the pinnacles far and free –
Up domes – up spires – up kingly halls –
Up fanes – up Babylon-like walls –
Up shadowy long-forgotten bowers
Of sculptured ivy and stone flowers –
Up many and many a marvellous shrine
Whose wreathed friezes intertwine
The viol, the violet, and the vine.
Resignedly beneath the sky
The melancholy waters lie.
So blend the turrets and shadows there
That all seem pendulous in air,
While from a proud tower in the town
Death looks gigantically down.
There open fanes and gaping graves
Yawn level with the luminous waves;
But not the riches there that lie
In each idol's diamond eye –
Not the gayly-jeweled dead
Tempt the waters from their bed;
For no ripples curl, alas!
Along that wilderness of glass –
No swellings tell that winds may be
Upon some far-off happier sea –
No heavings hint that winds have been
On seas less hideously serene.

But lo, a stir is in the air!
The wave – there is a movement there!
As if the towers had thrust aside,
In slightly sinking, the dull tide –
As if their tops had feebly given

A void within the filmy Heaven.
The waves have now a redder glow –
The hours are breathing faint and low –
And when, amid no earthly moans,
Down, down that town shall settle hence,
Hell, rising from a thousand thrones,
Shall do it reverence.

The Haunted Palace

In the greenest of our valleys
    By good angels tenanted,
Once a fair and stately palace –
    Radiant palace – reared its head.
In the monarch Thought's dominion –
    It stood there!
Never seraph spread a pinion
    Over fabric half so fair!

Banners yellow, glorious, golden,
    On its roof did float and flow,
(This – all this – was in the olden
    Time long ago,)
And every gentle air that dallied,
    In that sweet day,
Along the ramparts plumed and pallid,
    A winged odour went away.

Wanderers in that happy valley,
    Through two luminous windows, saw
Spirits moving musically,
    To a lute's well-tunéd law,
Round about a throne where, sitting,
    Porphyrogene,
In state his glory well befitting,
    The ruler of the realm was seen.

And all with pearl and ruby glowing

Was the fair palace door,
Through which came flowing, flowing, flowing,
And sparkling evermore,
A troop of Echoes, whose sweet duty
Was but to sing,
In voices of surpassing beauty,
The wit and wisdom of their king.

But evil things, in robes of sorrow,
Assailed the monarch's high estate.
(Ah, let us mourn! – for never morrow
Shall dawn upon him, desolate!)
And round about his home the glory
That blushed and bloomed
Is but a dim-remembered story
Of the old-time entombed.

And travellers, now, within that valley,
Through the encrimson'd windows see
Vast forms that move fantastically
To a discordant melody,
While, like a ghastly rapid river,
Through the pale door
A hideous throng rush out forever
And laugh – but smile no more.

ALFRED, LORD TENNYSON
born 6 August 1809 : died 6 October 1892

*The Kraken**

Below the thunders of the upper deep;
Far, far beneath in the abysmal sea,

* a fabled sea-monster

His ancient, dreamless, uninvaded sleep
The Kraken sleepeth: faintest sunlights flee
About his shadowy sides: above him swell
Huge sponges of millennial growth and height;
And far away into the sickly light,
From many a wondrous grot and secret cell
Unnumbered and enormous polypi
Winnow with giant arms the slumbering green.
There hath he lain for ages and will lie
Battening upon huge seaworms in his sleep,
Until the latter fire shall heat the deep;
Then once by man and angels to be seen,
In roaring he shall rise and on the surface die.

The Lady of Shalott

Part One

On either side the river lie
Long fields of barley and of rye,
That clothe the wold and meet the sky;
And through the field the road runs by
      To many-towered Camelot;
And up and down the people go,
Gazing where the lilies blow
Round an island there below,
      The island of Shalott.

Willows whiten, aspens quiver,
Little breezes dusk and shiver
Through the wave that runs for ever
By the island in the river
      Flowing down to Camelot.
Four gray walls, and four gray towers,
Overlook a space of flowers,
And the silent isle imbowers
      The Lady of Shalott.

By the margin, willow-veiled,

Slide the heavy barges trailed
By slow horses; and unhailed
The shallop flitteth silken-sailed
    Skimming down to Camelot:
But who hath seen her wave her hand?
Or at the casement seen her stand?
Or is she known in all the land,
    The Lady of Shalott?

Only reapers, reaping early
In among the bearded barley,
Hear a song that echoes cheerly
From the river winding clearly,
    Down to towered Camelot:
And by the moon the reaper weary,
Piling sheaves in uplands airy,
Listening, whispers ''Tis the fairy
    Lady of Shalott.'

Part Two

There she weaves by night and day
A magic web with colours gay.
She has heard a whisper say,
A curse is on her if she stay
    To look down to Camelot.
She knows not what the curse may be,
And so she weaveth steadily,
And little other care hath she,
    The Lady of Shalott.

And moving through a mirror clear
That hangs before her all the year,
Shadows of the world appear.
There she sees the highway near
    Winding down to Camelot:
There the river eddy whirls,
And there the surly village-churls,
And the red cloaks of market girls,
    Pass onward from Shalott.

Sometimes a troop of damsels glad,
An abbot on an ambling pad,
Sometimes a curly shepherd-lad,
Or long-haired page in crimson clad,
    Goes by to towered Camelot;
And sometimes through the mirror blue
The knights come riding two and two:
She hath no loyal knight and true,
    The Lady of Shalott.

But in her web she still delights
To weave the mirror's magic sights,
For often through the silent nights
A funeral, with plumes and lights
    And music, went to Camelot:
Or when the moon was overhead,
Came two young lovers lately wed;
'I am half sick of shadows,' said
    The Lady of Shalott.

Part Three

A bow-shot from her bower-eaves,
He rode between the barley-sheaves,
The sun came dazzling through the leaves,
And flamed upon the brazen greaves
    Of bold Sir Lancelot.
A red-cross knight for ever kneeled
To a lady in his shield,
That sparkled on the yellow field,
    Beside remote Shalott.

The gemmy bridle glittered free,
Like to some branch of stars we see
Hung in the golden Galaxy.
The bridle bells rang merrily
    As he rode down to Camelot:
And from his blazoned baldric slung
A mighty silver bugle hung,
And as he rode his armour rung,

Beside remote Shalott.

All in the blue unclouded weather
Thick-jewelled shone the saddle-leather,
The helmet and the helmet-feather
Burned like one burning flame together,
As he rode down to Camelot.
As often through the purple night,
Below the starry clusters bright,
Some bearded meteor, trailing light,
Moves over still Shalott.

His broad clear brow in sunlight glowed;
On burnished hooves his war-horse trode;
From underneath his helmet flowed
His coal-black curls as on he rode,
As he rode down to Camelot.
From the bank and from the river
He flashed into the crystal mirror,
'Tirra lirra,' by the river
Sang Sir Lancelot.

She left the web, she left the loom,
She made three paces through the room,
She saw the water-lily bloom,
She saw the helmet and the plume,
She looked down to Camelot.
Out flew the web and floated wide;
The mirror cracked from side to side;
'The curse is come upon me,' cried
The Lady of Shalott.

Part Four

In the stormy east-wind straining,
The pale yellow woods were waning,
The broad stream in his banks complaining.
Heavily the low sky raining
Over towered Camelot;
Down she came and found a boat

Beneath a willow left afloat,
And round about the prow she wrote
The Lady of Shalott.

And down the river's dim expanse
Like some bold seer in a trance,
Seeing all his own mischance –
With a glassy countenance
Did she look to Camelot.
And at the closing of the day
She loosed the chain, and down she lay;
The broad stream bore her far away,
The Lady of Shalott.

Lying, robed in snowy white
That loosely flew to left and right –
The leaves upon her falling light –
Through the noises of the night
She floated down to Camelot:
And as the boat-head wound along
The willowy hills and fields among,
They heard her singing her last song,
The Lady of Shalott.

Heard a carol, mournful, holy,
Chanted loudly, chanted lowly,
Till her blood was frozen slowly,
And her eyes were darkened wholly,
Turned to towered Camelot.
For ere she reached upon the tide
The first house by the water-side,
Singing in her song she died,
The Lady of Shalott.

Under tower and balcony,
By garden-wall and gallery,
A gleaming shape she floated by,
Dead-pale between the houses high,
Silent into Camelot.
Out upon the wharfs they come,

Knight and burgher, lord and dame,
And round the prow they read her name,
The Lady of Shalott.

Who is this? and what is here?
And in the lighted palace near
Died the sound of royal cheer;
And they crossed themselves for fear,
All the knights at Camelot:
But Lancelot mused a little space;
He said, 'She has a lovely face;
God in his mercy lend her grace,
The Lady of Shalott.'

SIR SAMUEL FERGUSON
born 10 March 1810 : died 9 August 1886

The Fairy Thorn

'Get up, our Anna dear, from the weary spinning-wheel;
For your father's on the hill, and your mother is asleep:
Come up above the crags, and we'll dance a highland reel
Around the fairy thorn on the steep.'

At Anna Grace's door 'twas thus the maidens cried,
Three merry maidens fair in kirtles of the green;
And Anna laid the rock and the weary wheel aside,
The fairest of the four, I ween.

They're glancing through the glimmer of the quiet eve,
Away in milky wavings of neck and ankle bare;
The heavy-sliding stream in its sleepy song they leave,
And the crags in the ghostly air:

And linking hand in hand, and singing as they go,
  The maids along the hillside have ta'en their fearless way,
Till they come to where the rowan trees in lonely beauty grow
  Beside the Fairy Hawthorn grey.

The Hawthorn stands between the ashes tall and slim,
  Like matron with her twin grand-daughters at her knee;
The rowan berries cluster o'er her low head grey and dim
  In ruddy kisses sweet to see.

The merry maidens four have ranged them in a row,
  Between each lovely couple a stately rowan stem,
And away in mazes wavy, like skimming birds they go,
  Oh, never caroll'd bird like them!

But solemn is the silence of the silvery haze
  That drinks away their voices in echoless repose,
And dreamily the evening has still'd the haunted braes
  And dreamier the gloaming grows.

And sinking one by one, like lark-notes from the sky
  When the falcon's shadow saileth across the open shaw,
Are hush'd the maidens' voices, as cowering down they lie
  In the flutter of their sudden awe.

For, from the air above, and the grassy ground beneath,
  And from the mountain-ashes and the old Whitethorn between,
A Power of faint enchantment doth through their beings breathe,
  And they sink down together on the green.

They sink together silent, and stealing side by side,
  They fling their lovely arms o'er their drooping necks so fair,
Then vainly strive again their naked arms to hide,
  For their shrinking necks again are bare.

Thus clasp'd and prostrate all, with their heads together bow'd,
  Soft o'er their bosoms' beating – the only human sound –
They hear the silky footsteps of the silent fairy crowd,
  Like a river in the air, gliding round.

No scream can any raise, no prayer can any say,
But wild, wild, the terror of the speechless three –
For they feel fair Anna Grace drawn silently away,
By whom they dare not look to see.

They feel their tresses twine with her parting locks of gold,
And the curls elastic falling, as her head withdraws;
They feel her sliding arms from their tranced arms unfold,
But they may not look to see the cause:

For heavy on their senses the faint enchantment lies
Through all that night of anguish and perilous amaze;
And neither fear nor wonder can ope their quivering eyes
Or their limbs from the cold ground raise,

Till out of night the earth has roll'd her dewy side,
With every haunted mountain and streamy vale below;
When, as the mist dissolves in the yellow morning tide,
The maidens' trance dissolveth so.

Then fly the ghastly three as swiftly as they may,
And tell their tale of sorrow to anxious friends in vain –
They pined away and died within the year and day,
And ne'er was Anna Grace seen again.

WILLIAM ALLINGHAM
born 19 March 1824 : died 18 November 1889

The Fairies

Up the airy mountain,
Down the rushy glen,
We daren't go a-hunting
For fear of little men;
Wee folk, good folk,

Trooping all together;
Green jacket, red cap,
And white owl's feather.

Down along the rocky shore
Some make their home,
They live on crispy pancakes
Of yellow tide-foam;
Some in the reeds
Of the black mountain lake,
With frogs for their watch-dogs,
All night awake.

High on the hill-top
The old King sits;
He is now so old and gray
He's nigh lost his wits.
With a bridge of white mist
Columbkill he crosses,
On his stately journeys
From Slieveleague to Rosses;
Or going up with music
On cold starry nights,
To sup with the Queen
Of the gay Northern Lights.

They stole little Bridget
For seven years long;
When she came down again
Her friends were all gone.
They took her lightly back,
Between the night and morrow,
They thought that she was fast asleep,
But she was dead with sorrow.
They have kept her ever since
Deep within the lake,
On a bed of flag-leaves,
Watching till she wake.

By the craggy hill-side,

Through the mosses bare,
They have planted thorn-trees
For pleasure here and there.
Is any man so daring
As dig them up in spite,
He shall find their sharpest thorns
In his bed at night.

Up the airy mountain,
Down the rushy glen,
We daren't go a-hunting
For fear of little men;
Wee folk, good folk,
Trooping all together;
Green jacket, red cap,
And white owl's feather.

SYDNEY THOMPSON DOBELL
born 5 April 1824 : died 22 August 1874

The Ballad of Keith of Ravelston

The murmur of the mourning ghost
That keeps the shadowy kine,
'O, Keith of Ravelston,
The sorrows of thy line!'

Ravelston, Ravelston,
The merry path that leads
Down the golden morning hill,
And thro' the silver meads;

Ravelston, Ravelston,
The stile beneath the tree,
The maid that kept her mother's kine
The song that sang she!

She sang her song, she kept her kine,
  She sat beneath the thorn
When Andrew Keith of Ravelston
  Rode thro' the Monday morn.

His hencemen sing, his hawk-bells ring,
  His belted jewels shine;
O, Keith of Ravelston,
  The sorrows of thy line!

Year after year, where Andrew came,
  Comes evening down the glade,
And still there sits a moonshine ghost
  Where sat the sunshine maid.

Her misty hair is faint and fair,
  She keeps the shadowy kine;
O, Keith of Ravelston,
  The sorrows of thy line!

I lay my hand upon the stile,
  The stile is lone and cold,
The burnie that goes babbling by
  Says naught that can be told.

Yet, stranger! here, from year to year,
  She keeps her shadowy kine;
O, Keith of Ravelston,
  The sorrows of thy line!

Step out three steps, where Andrew stood –
  Why blanch thy cheeks for fear?
The ancient stile is not alone,
  'Tis not the burn I hear!

She makes her immemorial moan,
  She keeps her shadowy kine;
O, Keith of Ravelston,
  The sorrows of thy line!

GEORGE MACDONALD
born 10 December 1824 : died 18 September 1905

Mammon Marriage

The croak of a raven hoar!
  A dog's howl, kennel-tied!
Loud shuts the carriage-door:
  The two are away on their ghastly ride
To Death's salt shore!

Where are the love and the grace?
  The bridegroom is thirsty and cold!
The bride's skull sharpens her face!
  But the coachman is driving, jubilant, bold,
The devil's pace.

The horses shiver'd and shook
  Waiting gaunt and haggard
With sorry and evil look;
  But swift as a drunken wind they stagger'd
'Longst Lethe brook.

Long since, they ran no more;
  Heavily pulling they died
On the sand of the hopeless shore
  Where never swell'd or sank a tide,
And the salt burns sore.

Flat their skeletons lie,
  White shadows on shining sand;
The crusted reins go high
  To the crumbling coachman's bony hand
On his knees awry.

Side by side, jarring no more,
  Day and night side by side,
Each by a doorless door,

Motionless sit the bridegroom and bride
On the Dead-Sea-shore.

GEORGE MEREDITH
born 12 February 1828 : died 18 May 1909

Will o' the Wisp

Follow me, follow me,
Over brake and under tree,
Thro' the bosky tanglery,
Brushwood and bramble!
Follow me, follow me,
Laugh and leap and scramble!
Follow, follow,
Hill and hollow,
Fosse and burrow,
Fen and furrow,
Down into the bulrush beds,
'Midst the reeds and osier heads,
In the rushy soaking damps,
Where the vapours pitch their camps,
Follow me, follow me,
For a midnight ramble!
O! what a mighty fog,
What a merry night O ho!
Follow, follow, nigher, nigher –
Over bank, and pond, and briar,
Down in the croaking ditches,
Rotten log,
Spotted frog,
Beetle bright
With crawling light,
What a joy O ho!
Deep into the purple bog –

What a joy O ho!
Where like hosts of puckered witches
All the shivering agues sit
Warming hands and chafing feet,
By the blue marsh-hovering oils:
O the fools for all their moans!
Not a forest mad with fire
Could still their teeth, or warm their bones,
Or loose them from their chilly coils.
What a clatter,
How they chatter!
Shrink and huddle,
All a muddle!
What a joy O ho!
Down we go, down we go,
What a joy O ho!
Soon shall I be down below,
Plunging with a grey fat friar,
Hither, thither, to and fro,
Breathing mists and whisking lamps,
Plashing in the slimy swamps;
While my cousin Lantern Jack,
With cock ears and cunning eyes,
Turns him round upon his back,
Daubs him oozy green and black,
Sits upon his rolling size,
Where he lies, where he lies,
Groaning full of sack –
Staring with his great round eyes!
What a joy O ho!
Sits upon him in the swamps
Breathing mists and whisking lamps!
What a joy O ho!
Such a lad is Lantern Jack,
When he rides the black nightmare
Through the fens, and puts a glare
In the friar's track.
Such a frolic lad, good lack!
To turn a friar on his back,
Trip him, clip him, whip him, nip him.

Lay him sprawling, smack!
Such a lad is Lantern Jack!
Such a tricksy lad, good lack!
What a joy O ho!
Follow me, follow me,
Where he sits, and you shall see!

DANTE GABRIEL ROSSETTI
born 12 May 1828 : died 9 April 1882

Sister Helen

'Why did you melt your waxen man',
Sister Helen?
Today is the third since you began.'
'The time was long, yet the time ran,
Little brother.'
(*O Mother, Mary Mother,*
Three days today, between Hell and Heaven!)

'But if you have done your work aright,
Sister Helen,
You'll let me play, for you said I might.'
'Be very still in your play tonight,
Little Brother.'
(*O Mother, Mary Mother,*
Third night, tonight, between Hell and Heaven!)

'You said it must melt ere vesper bell,
Sister Helen;
If now it be molten, all is well.'
'Even so, – nay, peace! you cannot tell,
Little Brother.'
(*O Mother, Mary Mother,*
O what is this, between Hell and Heaven?)

'Oh the waxen knave was plump today,
Sister Helen;
How like dead folk he has dropped away!'
'Nay now, of the dead what can you say,
Little brother?'
(*O Mother, Mary Mother,*
What of the dead, between Hell and Heaven?)

'See, see, the sunken pile of wood,
Sister Helen,
Shines through the thinned wax red as blood!'
'Nay now, when looked you yet on blood,
Little Brother?'
(*O Mother, Mary Mother,*
How pale she is, between Hell and Heaven!)

'Now close your eyes, for they're sick and sore,
Sister Helen,
And I'll play without the gallery door.'
'Aye, let me rest, – I'll lie on the floor,
Little Brother.'
(*O Mother, Mary Mother,*
What rest tonight, between Hell and Heaven?)

'Here high up in the balcony,
Sister Helen,
The moon flies face to face with me.'
'Aye, look and say whatever you see,
Little brother.'
(*O Mother, Mary Mother,*
What sight tonight, between Hell and Heaven?)

'Outside it's merry in the wind's wake,
Sister Helen;
In the shaken trees the chill stars shake.'
'Hush, heard you a horse-tread as you spake,
Little brother?'
(*O Mother, Mary Mother,*
What sound tonight, between Hell and Heaven?)

'I hear a horse-tread, and I see,
Sister Helen,
Three horsemen that ride terribly.'
'Little brother, whence come the three,
Little brother?'
(*O Mother, Mary Mother,*
Whence should they come, between Hell and Heaven?)

'They come by the hill-verge from Boyne Bar,
Sister Helen,
And one draws nigh, but two are afar.'
'Look, look, do you know them who they are,
Little brother?'
(*O Mother, Mary Mother,*
Who should they be, between Hell and Heaven?)

'Oh, it's Keith of Eastholm rides so fast,
Sister Helen,
For I know the white mane on the blast.'
'The hour has come, has come at last,
Little brother!'
(*O Mother, Mary Mother,*
Her hour at last, between Hell and Heaven!)

'He has made a sign and called Halloo!
Sister Helen,
And he says that he would speak with you.'
'Oh tell him I fear the frozen dew,
Little brother.'
(*O Mother, Mary Mother,*
Why laughs she thus, between Hell and Heaven?)

'The wind is loud, but I hear him cry,
Sister Helen,
That Keith of Ewern's like to die.'
'And he and thou, and thou and I,
Little brother.'
(*O Mother, Mary Mother,*
And they and we, between Hell and Heaven!)

'Three days ago, on his marriage-morn,
Sister Helen,
He sickened, and lies since then forlorn.'
'For bridegroom's side is the bride a thorn,
Little Brother?'
(*O Mother, Mary Mother,*
Cold bridal cheer, between Hell and Heaven!)

'Three days and nights he has lain abed,
Sister Helen,
And he prays in torment to be dead.'
'The thing may chance, if he have prayed,
Little brother!'
(*O Mother, Mary Mother,*
If he have prayed, between Hell and Heaven!)

'But he has not ceased to cry to-day,
Sister Helen,
That you should take your curse away.'
'*My* prayer was heard, – he need but pray,
Little brother!'
(*O Mother, Mary Mother,*
Shall God not hear, between Hell and Heaven?)

'But he says, till you take back your ban,
Sister Helen,
His soul would pass, yet never can.'
'Nay then, shall I slay a living man,
Little brother?'
(*O Mother, Mary Mother,*
A living soul, between Hell and Heaven!)

'But he calls for ever on your name,
Sister Helen,
And says that he melts before a flame.'
'My heart for his pleasure fared the same,
Little brother.'
(*O Mother, Mary Mother,*
Fire at the heart, between Hell and Heaven!)

'Here's Keith of Westholm riding fast,
Sister Helen,
For I know the white plume on the blast.'
'The hour, the sweet hour I forecast,
Little brother!'
(*O Mother, Mary Mother,*
Is the hour sweet, between Hell and Heaven?)

'He stops to speak, and he stills his horse,
Sister Helen;
But his words are drowned in the wind's course.'
'Nay hear, nay hear, you must hear perforce,
Little brother!'
(*O Mother, Mary Mother,*
What word now heard, between Hell and Heaven?)

'Oh he says that Keith of Ewern's cry,
Sister Helen,
Is ever to see you ere he die.'
'In all that his soul sees, there am I,
Little brother!'
(*O Mother, Mary Mother,*
The soul's one sight, between Hell and Heaven!)

'He sends a ring and a broken coin,
Sister Helen,
And bids you mind the banks of Boyne.'
'What else he broke will he ever join,
Little brother?'
(*O Mother, Mary Mother,*
No, never joined, between Hell and Heaven!)

'He yields you these and craves full fain,
Sister Helen,
You pardon him in his mortal pain.'
'What else he took will he give again,
Little brother?'
(*O Mother, Mary Mother,*
Not twice to give, between Hell and Heaven!)

'He calls your name in an agony,
Sister Helen,
That even dead Love must weep to see.'
'Hate, born of Love, is blind as he,
Little brother!'
(*O Mother, Mary Mother,*
Love turned to hate, between Hell and Heaven!)

'Oh it's Keith of Keith now that rides fast,
Sister Helen,
For I know the white hair on the blast.'
'The short short hour will soon be past,
Little brother!'
(*O Mother, Mary Mother,*
Will soon be past, between Hell and Heaven!)

'He looks at me and he tries to speak,
Sister Helen,
But oh! his voice is sad and weak!'
'What here should the mighty Baron seek,
Little brother?'
(*O Mother, Mary Mother,*
Is this the end, between Hell and Heaven?)

'Oh his son still cries, if you forgive,
Sister Helen,
The body dies but the soul shall live.'
'Fire shall forgive me as I forgive,
Little brother!'
(*O Mother, Mary Mother,*
As she forgives, between Hell and Heaven!)

'Oh he prays you, as his heart would rive,
Sister Helen,
To save his dear son's soul alive.'
'Fire cannot slay it, it shall thrive,
Little brother!'
(*O Mother, Mary Mother,*
Alas, alas, between Hell and Heaven!)

'He cries to you, kneeling in the road,
Sister Helen,
To go with him for the love of God!'
'The way is long to his son's abode,
Little brother.'
(*O Mother, Mary Mother,*
The way is long, between Hell and Heaven!)

'A lady's here, by a dark steed brought,
Sister Helen,
So darkly clad, I saw her not.'
'See her now or never see aught,
Little brother!'
(*O Mother, Mary Mother,*
What more to see, between Hell and Heaven?)

'Her hood falls back, and the moon shines fair,
Sister Helen,
On the Lady of Ewern's golden hair.'
'Blest hour of my power and her despair,
Little brother!'
(*O Mother, Mary Mother,*
Hour blest and bann'd, between Hell and Heaven!)

'Pale, pale her cheeks, that in pride did glow,
Sister Helen,
'Neath the bridal-wreath three days ago.'
'One morn for pride and three days of woe,
Little brother!'
(*O Mother, Mary Mother,*
Three days, three nights, between Hell and Heaven!)

'Her clapsed hands stretch from her bending head,
Sister Helen;
With the loud wind's wail her sobs are wed.'
'What wedding-strains hath her bridal-bed,
Little brother?'
(*O Mother, Mary Mother,*
What strain but death's, between Hell and Heaven!)

'She may not speak, she sinks in a swoon,
Sister Helen, –
She lifts her lips and gasps on the moon.'
'Oh! might I but hear her soul's blithe tune,
Little brother!'
(*O Mother, Mary Mother,*
Her woe's dumb cry, between Hell and Heaven!)

'They've caught her to Westholm's saddle-bow,
Sister Helen,
And her moonlit hair gleams white in its flow.'
'Let it turn whiter than winter snow,
Little brother!'
(*O Mother, Mary Mother,*
Woe-withered gold, between Hell and Heaven!)

'O Sister Helen, you heard the bell.
Sister Helen!
More loud than the vesper-chime it fell.'
'No vesper-chime, but a dying knell,
Little brother!'
(*O Mother, Mary Mother,*
His dying knell, between Hell and Heaven!)

'Alas! but I fear the heavy sound,
Sister Helen;
Is it in the sky or in the ground?'
'Say, have they turned their horses round,
Little brother?'
(*O Mother, Mary Mother,*
What would she more, between Hell and Heaven?)

'They have raised the old man from his knee,
Sister Helen,
And they ride in silence hastily.'
'More fast the naked soul doth flee,
Little brother!'
(*O Mother, Mary Mother,*
The naked soul, between Hell and Heaven!)

'Flank to flank are the three steeds gone,
Sister Helen,
But the lady's dark steed goes alone.'
'And lonely her bridegroom's soul hath flown,
Little brother.'
(*O Mother, Mary Mother,*
The lonely ghost, between Hell and Heaven!)

'Oh the wind is sad in the iron chill,
Sister Helen,
And weary sad they look by the hill.'
'But he and I are sadder still,
Little brother!'
(*O Mother, Mary Mother,*
Most sad of all, between Hell and Heaven!)

'See, see, the wax has dropped from its place,
Sister Helen,
And the flames are winning up apace!'
'Yet here they burn but for a space,
Little brother!'
(*O Mother, Mary Mother,*
Here for a space, between Hell and Heaven!)

'Ah! what white thing at the door has cross'd,
Sister Helen?
Ah! what is this that sighs in the frost?'
'A soul that's lost as mine is lost,
Little brother!'
(*O Mother, Mary Mother,*
Lost, lost, all lost, between Hell and Heaven!)

CHRISTINA GEORGINA ROSSETTI
born 5 December 1830 : died 29 December 1894

The Hour and the Ghost

BRIDE
O love, love, hold me fast,
He draws me away from thee;
I cannot stem the blast,
Nor the cold strong sea:
Far away a light shines
Beyond the hills and pines;
It is lit for me.

BRIDEGROOM
I have thee close, my dear,
No terror can come near;
Only far off the northern light shines clear.

GHOST
Come with me, fair and false,
To our home, come home.
It is my voice that calls:
Once thou wast not afraid
When I woo'd, and said,
'Come, our nest is newly made' –
Now cross the tossing foam.

BRIDE
Hold me one moment longer,
He taunts me with the past,
His clutch is waxing stronger,
Hold me fast, hold me fast.
He draws me from thy heart,
And I cannot withhold:
He bids my spirit depart
With him into the cold: –
Oh bitter vows of old!

BRIDEGROOM
Lean on me, hide thine eyes:
Only ourselves, earth and skies,
Are present here: be wise.

GHOST
Lean on me, come away,
I will guide and steady:
Come, for I will not stay:
Come, for house and bed are ready.
Ah, sure bed and house,
For better and worse, for life and death:
Goal won with shortened breath:
Come, crown our vows.

BRIDE
One moment, one more word,
While my heart beats still,
While my breath is stirred
By my fainting will.
O friend forsake me not,
Forget not as I forgot:
But keep thy heart for me,
Keep thy faith true and bright;
Through the lone cold winter night
Perhaps I may come to thee.

BRIDEGROOM
Nay peace, my darling, peace:
Let these dreams and terrors cease:
Who spoke of death or change or aught but ease?

GHOST
O fair frail sin,
O poor harvest gathered in!
Thou shalt visit him again
To watch his heart grow cold;
To know the gnawing pain
I knew of old;
To see one much more fair

Fill up the vacant chair,
Fill his heart, his children bear: –
While thou and I together
In the outcast weather
Toss and howl and spin.

OWEN MEREDITH: 1st Earl of Lytton
born 8 November 1831 : died 24 November 1891

Saturnalia

Hid in the heaviest dark, a mystery
   Within a mystery, the sea augments
Night's witchcraft with its shadowy sound; the sigh
   Of an uneasy silence, that half vents
In sobs and gasps the dreadful secrecy
         Of its contents!

And yet another mystery haunts the night:
   The uncouth, phantasmal, bodiless return
Of Chaos. That which was before the light
   Comes back when light departs, and the deep urn
Of darkness voids confusions infinite
         That seethe and yearn.

All spectres now resume their dim domain.
   A shrouded dream is passing o'er the deep.
The scatter'd clusters of effaced stars wane
   Behind a livid film. The shuddering heap
Of waters hoarser breathes. Athwart my brain
         Vast shadows sweep.

My waking self sinks from me. In its place
   There comes a sense of preternatural force
Freed from thought's timid tyranny. The chase

Begins. The phantom bugles blow. To horse!
I mount the Nightmare. Flee thro' time and space
Speeds our wild course!

Where are we hurrying, they and I? And they,
Who are they? We shall find each other out
As we go on, perhaps, and by the way
Discover also what we are about.
Heavens! Is it you? How came you here astray
In such a rout?

They told me you were settled down in life,
Well married, living far away from here
In your own country, a good happy wife
And mother, virtue's model, a sincere
Church-goer, all whose decent days were rife
With heavenly cheer.

Yet here you are tonight, without a blush,
Stark naked, riding furious at my side
The Devil's own charger! Foremost in the push
Of this fierce crowd, and no attempt to hide
Your unashamed enjoyment of the rush
Of our wild ride!

Who is it you were laughing with just now
Before you join'd me? The tall woman there,
With the gold fillet glittering on her brow,
And those large long-lash'd eyes, and bosoms bare?
What is it hanging from her saddle bow
By a tress of hair?

Stay! Now she has it in her hands. It is
A dead man's head. And how her burning eyes
Gloat on its horror! How her red lips kiss
Those white ones! Yes, 'tis she, I recognize
Herodias. But you never told me this.
Who could surmise

That you were old associates? And you,

Whom have you loved to death, that you should be
Here in such company? Yon couple, too?
She with the man asleep upon her knee?
Asleep, or dead? A nail is driven thro'
His forehead. See!

With what still rapture her white fingers rove
Among his matted curls, as low she bends
Her glowing gaze his upturn'd face above,
Husht as a watchful mother when she tends
Her sick child, lull'd to sleep with songs of love!
So you are friends?

I noticed that the woman, as we pass'd,
Nodded to you encouragingly. Drums
And cymbals! Hark! Behind us prancing fast,
Here, with the head of Holofernes, comes
Dame Judith, bravely dress'd! And now, the vast
Black midnight hums

With a mysterious far-off music. Songs
Unholy, soft lascivious Lydian lyres,
Shrill Phrygian pipes, and throbbing Scythian gongs,
In wizard concert where, round monstrous fires,
The redden'd gloom reveals dim dancing throngs,
And loose-robed choirs.

O hasten! Hasten! If we get not there
Before the dawn breaks, we shall be undone!
Our steeds flag, and we still have far to fare.
Flog the jade fast! The revel has begun.
Faster! Our names are call'd. Death and despair!
Too late ... the Sun!

WILLIAM MORRIS
born 24 March 1834 : died 3 October 1896

The Writing on the Image

Argument.
How on an Image that stood anciently in Rome were written certain words, which none understood, until a Scholar, coming there, knew their meaning, and thereby discovered great marvels, but withal died miserably.

In half-forgotten days of old,
As by our fathers we were told,
Within the town of Rome there stood
An image cut of cornel wood,
And on the upraised hand of it
Men might behold these letters writ –
'PERCUTE HIC:' which is to say,
In that tongue that we speak today,
'*Strike here*!' nor yet did any know
The cause why this was written so.

Thus in the middle of the square,
In the hot sun and summer air,
The snow-drift and the driving rain,
That image stood, with little pain,
For twice a hundred years and ten;
While many a band of striving men
Were driven betwixt woe and mirth
Swiftly across the weary earth,
From nothing unto dark nothing:
And many an Emperor and King,
Passing with glory or with shame,
Left little record of his name,
And no remembrance of the face
Once watched with awe for gifts or grace.
Fear little, then, I counsel you,

What any son of man can do;
Because a log of wood will last
While many a life of man goes past,
And all is over in short space.

Now so it chanced that to this place
There came a man of Sicily,
Who when the image he did see,
Knew full well who, in days of yore,
Had set it there; for much strange lore,
In Egypt and in Babylon,
This man with painful toil had won;
And many secret things could do;
So verily full well he knew
That master of all sorcery
Who wrought the thing in days gone by,
And doubted not that some great spell
It guarded, but could nowise tell
What it might be. So, day by day,
Still would he loiter on the way,
And watch the image carefully,
Well mocked of many a passer-by.
And on a day he stood and gazed
Upon the slender finger, raised
Against a doubtful cloudy sky,
Nigh noontide; and thought, 'Certainly
The master who made thee so fair
By wondrous art, had not stopped there,
But made thee speak, had he not thought
That thereby evil might be brought
Upon his spell.' But as he spoke,
From out a cloud the noon sun broke
With watery light, and shadows cold:
Then did the Scholar well behold
How, from that finger carved to tell
Those words, a short black shadow fell
Upon a certain spot of ground,
And thereon, looking all around
And seeing none heeding, went straightway
Whereas the finger's shadow lay,

And with his knife about the place
A little circle did he trace;
Then home he turned with throbbing head,
And forthright gat him to his bed,
And slept until the night was late
And few men stirred from gate to gate.
So when at midnight he did wake,
Pickaxe and shovel did he take,
And, going to that now silent square,
He found the mark his knife made there,
And quietly with many a stroke
The pavement of the place he broke:
And so, the stones being set apart,
He 'gan to dig with beating heart,
And from the hole in haste he cast
The marl and gravel; till at last,
Full shoulder high, his arms were jarred,
For suddenly his spade struck hard
With clang against some metal thing:
And soon he found a brazen ring,
All green with rust, twisted, and great
As a man's wrist, set in a plate
Of copper, wrought all curiously
With words unknown though plain to see,
Spite of the rust: and flowering trees,
And beasts, and wicked images,
Whereat he shuddered: for he knew
What ill things he might come to do,
If he should still take part with these
And that Great Master strive to please.
But small time had he then to stand
And think, so straight he set his hand
Unto the ring, but where he thought
That by main strength it must be brought
From out its place, lo! easily
It came away, and let him see
A winding staircase wrought of stone,
Where through the new-come wind did moan.
Then thought he, 'If I come alive
From out this place well shall I thrive,

For I may look here certainly
The treasures of a king to see,
A mightier man than men are now.
So in few days what man shall know
The needy Scholar, seeing me
Great in the place where great men be,
The richest man in all the land?
Beside the best then shall I stand,
And some unheard-of palace have;
And if my soul I may not save
In heaven, yet here in all men's eyes
Will I make some sweet paradise,
With marble cloisters, and with trees
And bubbling wells, and fantasies,
And things all men deem strange and rare,
And crowds of women kind and fair,
That I may see, if so I please,
Laid on the flowers, or mid the trees
With half-clad bodies wandering.
There, dwelling happier than the king,
What lovely days may yet be mine!
How shall I live with love and wine,
And music, till I come to die!
And then – Who knoweth certainly
What haps to us when we are dead?
Truly I think by likelihead
Nought haps to us of good or bad;
Therefore on earth will I be glad
A short space, free from hope or fear;
And fearless will I enter here
And meet my fate, whatso it be.'

Now on his back a bag had he,
To bear what treasure he might win,
And therewith now did he begin
To go adown the winding stair;
And found the walls all painted fair
With images of many a thing,
Warrior and priest, and queen and king,
But nothing knew what they might be.

Which things full clearly could he see,
For lamps were hung up here and there
Of strange device, but wrought right fair,
And pleasant savour came from them.
At last a curtain, on whose hem
Unknown words in red gold were writ,
He reached, and softly raising it
Stepped back, for now did he behold
A goodly hall hung round with gold,
And at the upper end could see
Sitting, a glorious company:
Therefore he trembled, thinking well
They were no men, but fiends of hell.
But while he waited, trembling sore,
And doubtful of his late-learned lore,
A cold blast of the outer air
Blew out the lamps upon the stair
And all was dark behind him; then
Did he fear less to face those men
Than, turning round, to leave them there
While he went groping up the stair.
Yea, since he heard no cry or call
Or any speech from them at all,
He doubted they were images
Set there some dying king to please
By that Great Master of the art;
Therefore at last with stouter heart
He raised the cloth and entered in
In hope that happy life to win,
And drawing nigher did behold
That these were bodies dead and cold
Attired in full royal guise,
And wrought by art in such a wise
That living they all seemed to be,
Whose very eyes he well could see,
That now beheld not foul or fair,
Shining as though alive they were.
And midmost of that company
An ancient king that man could see,
A mighty man, whose beard of grey

A foot over his gold gown lay;
And next beside him sat his queen
Who in a flowery gown of green
And golden mantle well was clad,
And on her neck a collar had
Too heavy for her dainty breast;
Her loins by such a belt were prest
That whoso in his treasury
Held that alone, a king might be.
On either side of these, a lord
Stood heedfully before the board,
And in their hands held bread and wine
For service; behind these did shine
The armour of the guards, and then
The well-attired serving-men,
The minstrels clad in raiment meet;
And over against the royal seat
Was hung a lamp, although no flame
Was burning there, but there was set
Within its open golden fret
A huge carbuncle, red and bright;
Wherefrom there shone forth such a light
That great hall was as clear by it
As though by wax it had been lit,
As some great church at Easter-tide.
   Now set a little way aside,
Six paces from the daïs stood
An image made of brass and wood,
In likeness of a full-armed knight
Who pointed 'gainst the ruddy light
A huge shaft ready in a bow.
   Pondering how he could come to know
What all these marvellous matters meant,
About the hall the Scholar went,
Trembling, though nothing moved as yet;
And for awhile did he forget
The longings that had brought him there
In wondering at these marvels fair;
And still for fear he doubted much
One jewel of their robes to touch.

But as about the hall he passed
He grew more used to them at last,
And thought, 'Swiftly the time goes by,
And now no doubt the day draws nigh;
Folk will be stirring: by my head
A fool I am to fear the dead,
Who have seen living things enow,
Whose very names no man can know,
Whose shapes brave men might well affright
More than the lion in the night
Wandering for food:' therewith he drew
Unto those royal corpses two,
That on dead brows still were the crown;
And midst the golden cups set down
The rugged wallet from his back,
Patched of strong leather, brown and black.
Then, opening wide its mouth, took up
From off the board, a golden cup
The King's dead hand was laid upon,
Whose unmoved eyes upon him shone
And recked no more of that last shame
Than if he were the beggar lame,
Who in old days was wont to wait
For a dog's meal beside the gate.
Of which shame nought our man did reck,
But laid his hand upon the neck
Of the slim Queen, and thence undid
The jewelled collar, that straight slid
Down her smooth bosom to the board.
And when these matters he had stored
Safe in his sack, with both their crowns,
The jewelled parts of their rich gowns,
Their shoes and belts, brooches and rings,
And cleared the board of all rich things,
He staggered with them down the hall.
But as he went his eyes did fall
Upon a wonderful green stone,
Upon the hall-floor laid alone;
He said, 'Though thou art not so great
To add by much unto the weight

Of this my sack indeed, yet thou,
Certes, would make me rich enow,
That verily with thee I might
Wage one-half of the world to fight
The other half of it, and I
The lord of all the world might die; –
I will not leave thee;' therewithal
He knelt down midmost of the hall,
Thinking it would come easily
Into his hand; but when that he
Gat hold of it, full fast it stack,
So fuming, down he laid his sack,
And with both hands pulled lustily,
But as he strained, he cast his eye
Unto the daïs, and saw there
The image who the great bow bare
Moving the bowstring to his ear;
So, shrieking out aloud for fear,
Of that rich stone he loosed his hold
And catching up his bag of gold,
Gat to his feet: but ere he stood
The evil thing of brass and wood
Up to his ear the notches drew;
And clanging, forth the arrow flew,
And midmost of the carbuncle
Clanging again, the forked barbs fell,
And all was dark as pitch straightway.
  So there until the judgment day
Shall come and find his bones laid low,
And raise them up for weal or woe,
This man must bide; cast down he lay
While all his past life day by day
In one short moment he could see
Drawn out before him, while that he
In terror by that fatal stone
Was laid, and scarcely dared to moan.
But in a while his hope returned,
And then, though nothing he discerned,
He gat him up upon his feet,
And all about the walls he beat

To find some token of the door,
But never could he find it more,
For by some dreadful sorcery
All was sealed close as it might be,
And midst the marvels of that hall
This Scholar found the end of all.

But in the town on that same night,
An hour before the dawn of light,
Such storm upon the place there fell,
That not the oldest man could tell
Of such another: and thereby
The image was burnt utterly,
Being stricken from the clouds above;
And folk deemed that same bolt did move
The pavement where that wretched one
Unto his foredoomed fate had gone,
Because the plate was set again
Into its place, and the great rain
Washed the earth down, and sorcery
Had hid the place where it did lie.
So soon the stones were set all straight,
But yet the folk, afraid of fate,
Where once the man of cornel wood
Through many a year of bad and good
Had kept his place, set up alone
Great Jove himself, cut in white stone,
But thickly overlaid with gold.
'Which,' saith my tale, 'you may behold
Unto this day, although indeed
Some Lord or other, being in need,
Took every ounce of gold away.'
But now, this tale in some past day
Being writ, I warrant all is gone,
Both gold and weather-beaten stone.

Be merry, masters, while ye may,
For men much quicker pass away.

from *The Earthly Paradise.*

ALGERNON CHARLES SWINBURNE
born 5 April 1837 : died 10 April 1909

After Death

The four boards of the coffin lid
Heard all the dead man did.

The first curse was in his mouth,
Made of grave's mould and deadly drouth.

The next curse was in his head,
Made of God's work discomfited.

The next curse was in his hands,
Made out of two grave-bands.

The next curse was in his feet,
Made out of a grave-sheet.

'I had fair coins red and white,
And my name was as great light;

I had fair clothes green and red,
And strong gold bound round my head.

But no meat comes in my mouth,
Now I fare as the worm doth;

And no gold binds in my hair
Now I fare as the blind fare.

My live thews were of great strength,
Now I am waxen a span's length;

My live sides were full of lust,
Now are they dried with dust.'

The first board spake and said:
'Is it best eating flesh or bread?'

The second answered it:
'Is wine or honey the more sweet?'

The third board spake and said:
'Is red gold worth a girl's gold head?'

The fourth made answer thus:
'All these things are as one with us.'

The dead man asked of them:
'Is the green land stained brown with flame?

Have they hewn my son for beasts to eat,
And my wife's body for beast's meat?

Have they boiled my maid in a brass pan,
And built a gallows to hang my man?'

The boards said to him:
'This is a lewd thing that ye deem.

Your wife has gotten a golden bed,
All the sheets are sewn with red.

Your son has gotten a coat of silk,
The sleeves are soft as curded milk.

Your maid has gotten a kirtle new,
All the skirt has braids of blue.

Your man has gotten both ring and glove,
Wrought well for eyes to love.'

The dead man answered thus:
'What good gift shall God give us?'

The boards answered him anon:
'Flesh to feed hell's worm upon.'

HENRY CLARENCE KENDALL

born 18 April 1839 : died 1 August 1882

Ghost Glen

'Shut your ears, stranger, or turn from Ghost Glen now,
For the paths are grown over, untrodden by men now;
Shut your ears, stranger,' saith the grey mother, crooning
Her sorcery runic, when sets the half-moon in.

To-night the north-easter goes travelling slowly,
But it never stoops down to that hollow unholy;
To-night it rolls loud on the ridges red-litten,
But it cannot abide in that forest, sin-smitten.

For over the pitfall the moon-dew is thawing,
And with never a body two shadows stand sawing –
The wraiths of two sawyers (step under and under),
Who did a foul murder and were blackened with thunder!

Whenever the storm-wind comes driven and driving,
Through the blood-spattered timber you may see the saw striving –
You may see the saw heaving, and falling, and heaving,
Whenever the sea-creek is chafing and grieving!

And across a burnt body, as black as an adder,
Sits the sprite of a sheep-dog (was ever sight sadder?)
For, as the dry thunder splits louder and faster,
The sprite of a sheep-dog howls for his master.

'Oh, count your beads deftly,' saith the grey mother, crooning
Her sorcery runic, when sets the half-moon in.
And well may she mutter, for the dark, hollow laughter
You will hear in the sawpits and the bloody logs after.

Aye, count your beads deftly, and keep your ways wary,
For the sake of the Saviour and sweet mother Mary.
Pray for your peace in those perilous places,
And pray for the laying of horrible faces.

One starts, with a forehead all wrinkled and livid,
Aghast at the lightnings sudden and vivid;
One telleth, with curses, the gold that they drew there
(Ah! cross your breast humbly) from him whom they slew there:

The stranger, who came from the loved, the romantic
Island that sleeps on the moaning Atlantic,
Leaving behind him a patient home, yearning
For the steps in the distance – never returning;

Who was left in the forest, shrunken and starkly,
Burnt by his slayers (so men have said, darkly),
With the half-crazy sheep-dog, who cowered beside there,
And yelled at the silence, and marvelled, and died there.

Yea, cross your breast humbly, and hold your breath tightly,
Or fly for your life from those shadows unsightly,
From the set staring features (cold, and so young, too),
And the death on the lips that a mother hath clung to.

I tell you, that bushman is braver than most men
Who even in daylight doth go through the Ghost Glen,
Although in that hollow unholy and lonely
He sees the dank sawpits and bloody logs only.

ANDREW LANG
born 31 March 1844 : died 20 July 1912

The Bridge of Death

'The dance is on the Bridge of Death
   And who will dance with me?'
'There's never a man of living men
   Will dare to dance with thee.'

Now Margaret's gone within her bower
  Put ashes in her hair,
And sackcloth on her bonnie breast,
  And on her shoulders bare.

There came a knock to her bower door,
  And blithe she let him in;
It was her brother from the wars,
  The dearest of her kin.

'Set gold within your hair, Margaret,
  Set gold within your hair;
And gold upon your girdle band,
  And on your breast so fair.

'For we are bidden to dance to-night,
  We may not bide away;
This one good night, this one fair night,
  Before the red new day.'

'Nay, no gold for my head, brother,
  Nay, no gold for my hair;
It is the ashes and dust of earth
  That you and I must wear.

'No gold work for my girdle band,
  No gold work on my feet;
But ashes of the fire, my love,
  But dust that the serpents eat.'

They danced across the Bridge of Death
  Above the black water,
And the marriage bell was tolled in hell
  For the souls of him and her.

EUGENE LEE-HAMILTON
born 6 January 1845 : died 7 September 1907

The Rising of the Dead

I saw a vast bare plain, and, overhead,
   A half-chilled sun that shed a sickly light;
   While far and wide, till out of reach of sight,
The earth's thin crust was heaving with the dead.

Who, as they struggled from their dusty bed,
   At first mere bones, by countless years made white,
   Took gradual flesh, and stood all huddled tight
In mute, dull groups, as yet too numb to dread.

And all the while the summoning trump on high
   With rolling thunder never ceased to shake
The livid vault of that unclouded sky,

Calling fresh hosts of skeletons to take
   Each his identity; until well-nigh
The whole dry worn-out earth appeared to wake.

The Binding of the Lost

In monstrous caverns, lit by the glare
   From pools of molten stone, the lost are pent
   In silent herds, – dim, shadowy, vaguely blent,
Yet each alone with his own black despair;

While, through the thickness of the lurid air,
   The flying fiends, from some far unseen vent,
   Bring on their bat-wing'd backs, in swift descent,
The souls who swell the waiting myriads there.

And then begins the binding of the lost
   With snaky thongs, before they be transferred

To realms of utter flame or utter frost;

And, like a sudden ocean boom, is heard,
  Uprising from the dim and countless host,
Pain's first vague roar, Hell's first wild useless word.

WILLIAM SHARP
born 12 September 1855 : died 14 December 1905

*The Willis-Dancers**

The moonlight floods the hollow dell: –
The dell where all the city's dead
Were laid, when oft the loud plague-bell
Filled wayfarers with sudden dread:
The accursëd plague it was that swept
The young from life, and spared the old –
Who wept and lived, and lived and wept
And mourned the silent sleepers in the dell's chill fold.

The hollow dell is fill'd with light,
The frosty radiance of the moon;
Yet gleams there are, more weirdly bright –
And what is that slow swelling tune?
It is not any wind that blows,
For not a wafted leaf doth fall;
What is the rustling sound that grows,
As if a low wind stirred amid the poplars tall?

Yon white, yon pale green hues that shine –
Are they but fungus-growths that beam:
What moves by yon funereal pine –
What haunts the pool where marsh-fires gleam?

* *The Willis-Dancers are the spirits of those who have died untimely, youths and maidens who on earth had no fulfilment of their desires. On certain nights they hold wild phantasmal revelry on earth.*

From out the shadow-haunted trees,
Along the nested hedgerows dumb,
And o'er the moonlit sloping leas
Singing a thin strange song the Willis-Dancers come.

In hurrying scores, with silent feet,
In weird processional array
They pass, with motions wild and fleet:
And now they gain the common way.
Adown the long white road they flit,
Slow-singing their unechoing song,
Till, where the Calvary, moonlit,
Crowns the low hill – round whose white base the dancers throng.

Fair, fair, unutterably fair,
With wild and gleaming eyes they pray
O for the breath of mortal air,
O for the joys grown faint and gray!
But never the carven god commands;
The frozen eyes nor gleam nor glance –
The Willis-folk ring phantom-hands,
Then laugh and mock and whirl away in frantic dance.

Wild, wild the dance, with blazing eyes,
With flowing hair, and faun-like leaps,
With thrilling shouts, and ecstasies.
Now one withdraws, and wails, and weeps:
Her grave-blanch'd hair around her thrown,
Her white hands claspt, she doth not hear
A voice that claims her for his own,
Nor hearkens her dead Lover call in awful fear.

For oft when from the grave they've fled
To gain phantasmal joys on earth –
Fair youth and maids who ne'er were wed
But died within their spring-time mirth –
A fearful thing hath happ'd to some:
A joyous dancer hath withdrawn,
Hath wailed and wept, and then grown numb,
And paled, and pass'd away ev'n as the stars at dawn.

The wan soul, with its burning gaze
From hollow eyes with anguish fill'd,
Would fain the lapsing maiden raise:
One moment all her being is thrilled
With one wild passionate desire –
Then, as a flame that is blown out
Or as a mist in the sun's fire,
She fades into the silence round the whirling rout.

Still wilder, swifter grows the fray:
Youths who on earth had lived in vain,
Maids who had yearned the livelong day
For ease to love's imperious pain,
All whose high hopes had come to nought,
All who for life's delights had striven,
All who had suffered, dreamt, or wrought
To make of our common Earth a glowing Heaven –

All, all, with eager, frantic haste
Swift dart and glide and dance and spring –
As gnats above a stagnant waste
Will interweave in a mazy ring –
With locks that once were living gold
Tossed wildly in the moonlit air,
With panting breasts that ne'er were cold
In the dear vanish'd days ere death came unaware:

Lovers who knew no joy of love
In the old barren years of life,
Together now enraptured move –
Claspt each to each with rapture rife:
Bosom to panting bosom pressed,
Hot lips athirst on thirsting lips,
Strange joys and languors doubly blest –
Snatch'd from the sombre grave, yea even from Death's eclipse!

Swift, swifter grows the mystic dance
More wild, more wild, each fierce embrace:
The woe of death's inheritance
Gleams ghastly on each wildered face:

A wan grey light illumes the head
Of the carv'd god to whom they prayed:
A halt – a hush – among the dead!
A long-drawn sigh – and lo, the Willis-Dancers fade!

FIONA MACLEOD*

The Washer of the Ford

There is a lonely stream afar in a lone dim land;
It hath white dust for shore it has, white bones
bestrew the strand:
The only thing that liveth there is a naked leaping
sword;
But I, who a seer am, have seen the whirling hand
Of the Washer of the Ford.

A shadowy shape of cloud and mist, of gloom and
dusk, she stands,
The Washer of the Ford:
She laughs, at times, and strews the dust through
the hollow of her hands.
She counts the sins of all men there, and slays
the red-stained horde –
The ghosts of all the sins of men must know the
whirling sword
Of the Washer of the Ford.

She stoops and laughs when in the dust she sees
a writhing limb:
'Go back into the ford,' she says, 'and hither and
thither swim;
Then I shall wash you white as snow, and shall
take you by the hand,

* *The pseudonym of William Sharp. See previous.*

And slay you there in silence with this my whirling
brand,
And trample you into the dust of this white,
windless sand.'
This is the laughing word
Of the Washer of the Ford
Along that silent strand.

WILLIAM BUTLER YEATS

born 13 June 1865 : died 28 January 1939

The Stolen Child

Where dips the rocky highland
Of Sleuth Wood in the lake,
There lies a leafy island
Where flapping herons wake
The drowsy water-rats;
There we've hid our faery vats,
Full of berries
And of reddest stolen cherries.
Come away, O human child!
To the waters and the wild
With a faery, hand in hand,
For the world's more full of weeping than
you can understand.

Where the wave of moonlight glosses
The dim grey sands with light,
Far off by furthest Rosses
We foot it all the night,
Weaving olden dances,
Mingling hands and mingling glances
Till the moon has taken flight;
To and fro we leap

And chase the frothy bubbles,
While the world is full of troubles
And is anxious in its sleep.
Come away, O human child!
To the waters and the wild
With a faery, hand in hand,
For the world's more full of weeping than
you can understand.

Where the wandering water gushes
From the hills above Glen-Car,
In pools among the rushes
That scarce could bathe a star,
We seek for slumbering trout
And whispering in their ears
Give them unquiet dreams;
Leaning softly out
From ferns that drop their tears
Over the young streams.
Come away, O human child!
To the waters and the wild
With a faery, hand in hand,
For the world's more full of weeping than
you can understand.

Away with us he's going,
The solemn-eyed:
He'll hear no more the lowing
Of the calves on the warm hillside
Or the kettle on the hob
Sing peace into his breast,
Or see the brown mice bob
Round and round the oatmeal-chest.
For he comes, the human child,
To the waters and the wild
With a faery, hand in hand,
From a world more full of weeping than
he can understand.

JOSEPH RUDYARD KIPLING
born 30 December 1865 : died 18 January 1936

The Sack of the Gods

'Strangers drawn from the ends of the earth, jewelled
    and plumed were we;
I was the Lord of the Inca Race, and she was the Queen
    of the Sea.
Under the stars beyond our stars where the reinless meteors glow,
Hotly we stormed Valhalla, a million years ago.

Dust of the stars was under our feet, glitter of stars above –
Wrecks of our wrath dropped reeling down as we fought and
    we spurned and we strove;
Worlds upon worlds we tossed aside, and scattered them
    to and fro,
The night that we stormed Valhalla, a million years ago.

She with the star I had marked for my own – I with my
    set desire –
Lost in the loom of the Night of Nights, 'wildered by worlds
    afire –
Met in a war 'twixt love and hate where the reinless meteors
    glow,
Hewing our way to Valhalla, a million years ago.'

from *The Naulahka*

WALTER DE LA MARE
born 25 April 1873 : died 22 June 1956

The Listeners

'Is there anybody there?' said the Traveller,
  Knocking on the moonlit door;
And his horse in the silence champed the grasses
  Of the forest's ferny floor:
And a bird flew up out of the turret,
  Above the Traveller's head:
And he smote upon the door again a second time;
  'Is there anybody there?' he said.
But no one descended to the Traveller;
  No head from the leaf-fringed sill
Leaned over and looked into his grey eyes,
  Where he stood perplexed and still.
But only a host of phantom listeners
  That dwelt in the lone house then
Stood listening in the quiet of the moonlight
  To that voice from the world of men:
Stood thronging the faint moonbeams on the dark stair,
  That goes down to the empty hall,
Hearkening in an air stirred and shaken
  By the lonely Traveller's call.
And he felt in his heart their strangeness,
  Their stillness answering his cry,
While his horse moved, cropping the dark turf,
  'Neath the starred and leafy sky;
For he suddenly smote on the door, even
  Louder, and lifted his head: –
'Tell them I came, and no one answered,
  That I kept my word,' he said.
Never the least stir made the listeners,
  Though every word he spake
Fell echoing through the shadowiness of the still house
  From the one man left awake:
Ay, they heard his foot upon the stirrup,

And the sound of iron on stone,
And how the silence surged softly backward,
When the plunging hoofs were gone.

JAMES ELROY FLECKER
born 5 November 1884 : died 3 January 1915

The Ballad of Zacho

Zacho the King rode out of old
(And truth is what I tell)
With saddle and spurs and a rein of gold
To find the door of Hell.

And round around him surged the dead
With soft and lustrous eyes.
'Why came you here, old friend?' they said:
'Unwise ... unwise ... unwise!

'You should have left to the prince your son
Spurs and saddle and rein:
Your bright and morning days are done;
You ride not out again.'

'I came to greet my friends who fell
Sword-scattered from my side;
And when I've drunk the wine of Hell
I'll out again and ride!'

But Charon rose and caught his hair
In fingers sharp and long.
'Loose me, old ferryman: play fair:
Try if my arm be strong.'

Thrice drave he hard on Charon's breast,

And struck him thrice to ground,
Till stranger ghosts came out o' the west
And sat like stars around.

And thrice old Charon rose up high
And seized him as before.
'Loose me! a broken man am I,
And fight with you no more.'

'Zacho, arise, my home is near;
I pray you walk with me:
I've hung my tent so full of fear
You well may shake to see.

'Home to my home come they who fight,
Who fight but not to win:
Without, my tent is black as night,
And red as fire within.

'Though winds blow cold and I grow old,
My tent is fast and fair:
The pegs are dead men's stout right arms,
The cords, their golden hair.'

FRANCIS LEDWIDGE
born 19 June 1891 : died 31 July 1917

The Shadow People

Old lame Bridget doesn't hear
Fairy music in the grass
When the gloaming's on the mere
And the shadow people pass:
Never hears their slow grey feet
Coming from the village street

Just beyond the parson's wall,
Where the clover globes are sweet
And the mushroom's parasol
Opens in the moonlit rain.
Every night I hear them call
From their long and merry train.
Old lame Bridget says to me,
'It is just your fancy, child.'
She cannot believe I see
Laughing faces in the wild,
Hands that twinkle in the sedge
Bowing at the water's edge
Where the finny minnows quiver,
Shaping on a blue wave's ledge
Bubble foam to sail the river.
And the sunny hands to me
Beckon ever, beckon ever.
Oh! I would be wild and free
And with the shadow people be.

GLOSSARY

Aboon: above
Affray: terrify
Ain: own
Airns: irons
Ake: ache
Alang: along
Ane: one
Aneath: beneath
Arles: pledges
Attour: above
Aye: always

Bairn: child
Baith: both
Bane: bone
Bear: barley
Bedesman: beadsman
Belive: quickly
Bewray: reveal
Birks: birches
Blawn: blown
Blellum: noisy fellow
Boddle: twopenny coin
Bogilis: hobgoblins
Bore: hole in a wall
Bottom of thrid: ball of thread
Bousing: drinking
Brainyell'd: stirred
Brake: broken
Brast: burst
Brawlie: perfectly
Breeks: breeches
Brent new: brand new
Brig: bridge
Brownyis: spirits
Bughts: milking pens
Burdies: girls
Byke: beehive

Cairn: burial stones
Cantrip: spell
Carle girn'd amain: old man snarled mightily
Carlin: old woman
Ca's a shoe: shed
Chapman billies: pedlars
Church-ale: church festival
Clatter: story-telling
Claught: caught
Cleekit: linked arms
Coft: bought
Coost her duddies: threw off her clothes
Corby: carrion crow
Cot: cottage
Cour: cower
Cranion: skull
Creeshie flannen: greasy flannel
Cruddy: clotted

Cummock: crooked staff
Cutty sark: short shirt

Deils: devils
Dirl: vibrate
Drouthy: thirsty
Dub: puddle

E'e: eye
Een: eye
Eident: diligent
Elyed: vanished
Ettle: intent

Fain: fond
Fairin': drubbing
Fand I nane: found I none
Faulds: sheepfolds
Fere: fellow
Fient: fiend
Flang: flung
Forhooy'd: forsook
Frae: from
Fyke: fuss

Gab: mouth
Gane: gone
Gars: causes
Gart: forced
Gate: road
Geck'd: mocked
Ghaists: ghosts
Gleid: glow
Gloaming: twilight
Goved: gazed
Gouden: golden
Gowl: roar
Gowl'd: roared
Greet: weep

Hale: whole
Hame: home
Happ'd: covered
Harn: coarse linen
Heft: handle
Herked: urged
Hindberrye: raspberry
Holt and den:
  hill and dell
Houf: haunt
Howlets: owlets
Hurdies: buttocks
Hypp: rosehip

Ilk: each
Ilka: every
Ingle: fireplace

Joup: petticoat

Kemed: combed
Kendna: did not know
Kenn'd: knew
Key-stane: keystone
Kirk: church
Kyth: appear

Laird: lord
Lane: alone
Lang: long
Lap: leaped
Leifu': wistful
Leme: flame
Lened: crouched
Libbards-bane:
  wolfbane herb
Linket: tripped deftly
Linn: waterfall
Littand: staining

Lowed: glowed
Lowping: jumping

Maike: companion
Mair: more
Maun: must
Mavis: thrush
Meikle: much
Melder: meal grinding
Merle: blackbird
Mess: Mass
Minny: mother
Mirk: dark
Mither: mother
Mooted: moulted

Nae: no
Naig: horse
Nappy: ale
Norland: northern
Nurice: nurse

Pund: pound
Pussie: hare

Queans: girls

Raike: wander
Rair: roar
Ramp: leap
Rape: rope
Reaming swats: foaming ale
Reek: smoke
Reekit: steamed
Rere-mice: bats
Rigwoodie: withered

Sae: so
Sair: sore
Sark: shirt
Scheen: sheen
Sey: attempt
Seymar: loose undergarment
Shaw: dell
Sic: such
Siller: silver
Skellum: rascal
Skelpit: hurried
Skirl: to shriek
Slaps: fence gaps
Smoor'd: smothered
Souter: shoemaker
Spean: wean
Speer: inquire
Stack: stuck
Swa'd: swelled
Swat: sweat
Swinked: struggled
Syne anither: then another

Ta'en: taken
Throstle-cock: missel-thrush
Tint: lost
Tippenny: ale
Tod: fox
Towzie tyke: shaggy dog
Twa: two

Unco: uncommonly
Unlich: unlike
Unmeled: unblemished
Usquabae: whisky

Vauntie: joyous

Wa': wall
Waik: grassy lane

Wain'd: carried
Walie: perfectly
Wark: work
Ween: believe
Weening: believing
Weir: war
Wene: dwelling
Westlin': western
Whins: furze-bushes
Winnock-bunker: window-seat
Wight: man
Wist: knew

Yorlin: yellow hammer